世界の空間デザイン
スペード

SPA-DE
SPACE & DESIGN

19

JAPAN SHOP 2013
ご来場ありがとうござました

3月5・6・7・8日の4日間開催「JAPAN SHOP2013」を盛況に終えることが出来ました。ご来場頂きました皆様、誠にありがとうございました。今回、「ベンジャミンムーアペイント ジャパン」にご協力頂き展示した **リブ 〜光と影と陰 ＋プラス 色彩** のご提案は大変ご好評頂きました。皆様にご活用頂けるリブの新しいご提案を今後も続けて参りたいと思います。
ご愛顧のほどよろしくお願い致します。

株式会社サカイ　社員一同

第5回 サカイリブを使ったデザインコンペ2015

開催決定!! 速報

詳しい応募要項は内容が固まり次第順次ホームページ上に
公開させて頂きます。今しばらくお待ちください。

募集概要 サカイリブを使い、実際に竣工した物件
当コンペ未応募の作品

応 募 エントリーシート準備中です!
今、しばらくお待ちください

締 切 2015年12月31日(大晦日)

審 査 施工写真による審査

発 表 2016年1月

副 賞 スリランカ+α 建築ツアー

第4回金賞「club PROUDIA」
サカイリブ ドレープ1200 design firm 2001 小坂和生 石山真子

金賞 1作品 銀賞 1作品 銅賞 2作品

審査員特別賞 5作品 優秀作品賞 10作品

〈審査員〉古谷 誠章(建築家・早稲田大学教授) 小坂 竜(インテリアデザイナー・(株)乃村工藝社A.N.D. 主宰)
橋本 夕紀夫(インテリアデザイナー・(有)橋本夕紀夫デザインスタジオ 代表)
鈴野 浩一(建築家・(株)トラフ建築設計事務所 共同主宰) 禿 真哉(建築家・(株)トラフ建築設計事務所 共同主宰)

株式会社サカイ賞 3作品 「収まり重視」主催者からの特別賞

受賞者には各賞に応じて賞金及び副賞(招待または参加権)が授与されます。

アッとおどろく使用方法、アイデアあふれる施工写真をお待ちしてます。

第3回アメリカ建築ツアー

第4回東欧建築ツアー

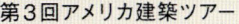

フリーダイヤル:0120-07-7810
URL:http://sakairib.com E-mail:sakairib@sakairib.com

Lightness.

豊かさをもたらす軽やかさ。

永井一正ポスター美術館
NAGAI KAZUMASA POSTER MUSEUM

NAGAI KAZUMASA POSTER MUSEUM　永井一正ポスター美術館

日本を代表するグラフィックデザイナー、永井一正のポスターの集大成。収録点数500点超保存版！

デジタル化した世の中におけるグラフィックデザイナーの可能性を語るインタビューを収録。

■ ソフトカバー・ジャケット装・B5 判変型 257×197mm・600 頁
■ ISBN978-4-89737-734-6
■ 定価：6,090 円（本体 5,800 円＋税）

株式会社 六耀社

〒160-0022 東京都新宿区新宿2-19-12 静岡銀行ビル
TEL: 03-3354-4020 ■ FAX: 03-3352-3106 ■ e-mail:books@rikuyosha.co.jp

SPA-DE Vol.19
CONTENTS

特集１：ライティング・グラフィックス
Feature 1: Lighting Graphics

010　Multi-purpose hall installation / **The Monsoon Club at Kennedy Centre**
Serie Architects

014　Restaurant and bar / **Clyde Frazier's Wine and Dine**
Morphosis

019　Culb / **D.Edge 2.0**
Muti Randolph

024　Skincare shop / **Aesop Twins; Aesop Westfield Bondi Junction and Aesop Westfield City Centre**
March Studio

028　Wallcovering Exhibition / **RGB**
Carnovsky

030　Concept Store / **NIKE + Fuelstation at Boxpark**
NIKE Brand Design Europe

032　Temporary restaurant / **Mi- Sha**
Simone Micheli

036　Sushi restaurant / **Yojisan Sushi**
Dan Brunn architect

特集２：ハイデザイン・フードショップ
Feature 2: Elaborately Designed Food Shops

040　Chocolate shop / **La Maison des Maîtres Chocolatiers**
Minale Design Strategy

044　Chocolate store / **Xocolatti**
de-spec Inc.

047　Premium olive oils store / **TA-ZE**
Burdifilek

050　Wine & Champagne bar / **Mistral Wine Store**
Studio Arthur Casas

055　Wine shop / **The Grapy Store**
Storeage

058　Boulangerie / **VyTA Boulangerie Italiana**
Daniela Colli

062　Frozen Yogurt Bar / **Froyo Yogurteria in Volos**
Ahylo Studio

066　Ice Cream Shop / **Ice Cream Castle**
Scenario Interior Architects

069　Café / **Coffee Bar**
jones | haydu

072　Belgian Fry Kiosk / **Bel Frites**
3six0 Architecture

074　Gourmet market / **EKI MARCHÉ OSAKA Marche's Kitchen and Entrée Marché Osaka**
Nomura Co.,Ltd

世界の空間デザイン
World Spatial Design

080　Theater / **Masrah Al Qasba Theatre**
magma architecture

085　Underground leisure lair and Public space / **Teruel-Zilla**
Mi5 arquitectos + PKMN architectures

090　Temporary showroom / **London 2012 BMW Group Pavilion**
Serie Architects

094　Museum / **Contemporary Art Museum (CAM) Raleigh**
Lawrence Scarpa

098　Cafeteria & Museum shop / **A Cantina**
Estudio Nômad

102　Temporary Showcase / **Nike Camp Victory**
Skylab Architecture

107　Installation / **Aesop Installation at I.T Hysan One**
Cheungvogl Architects

110　Bank / **Raiffeisen's flagship branch**
NAU together with Drexler Guinand Jauslin Architekten

114　Pharmacy / **Casanueva's Pharmacy**
Clavel Arquitectos

118　Medical Centre / **Edgecliff Medical Centre**
Patrick Keane

122　Gastromic reserch workshop / **Paco Roncero's workshop**
Carmen Baselga

126　Book store / **AKO books & travel**
Tjep

130　Pop-up hair salon / **Fudge Pop-up Hair Salon**
Zaha Hadid Architects

134　Hair salon / **Chalachol Hair Salon**
NKDW

138　Nightclub and Bar / **É Prá Poncha**
António Fernandez Architects

142　Take-away shop / **Eleven Inch Pizzeria**
Zwei Interiors Architecture

145　Boutique / **Nanushka Beta Store**
Daniel Balo, Zsofi Dobos, Dora Medveczky, Judit Emese Konopas, Noemi Varga

148　Shoe shop / **Shoebaloo Maastricht**
Meyer en Van Schooten Architecten (MVSA)

152　Pop up store / **Camper 20 years in Paris**
Studio François Dumas

156　Shoe shop / **Camper Steps**
Studio Makkink & Bey

160　Installation Architecture / **Sandworm**
Marco Casagrande

164　Designers and Architects' Portraits
165　Advertisement index　広告索引

Feature 1

Lighting Graphics

特集 1
ライティング・グラフィックス

空間デザインにおいて照明が重要な要素であることは、改めて言うまでもない。全般照明や局所照明、間接照明など、さまざまな照明テクニックの使い方で、得られる空間的効果は全く異なったものとなる。

また、照明は輝度や色彩といった視覚的に強い効果も持っている。それをグラフィカルに扱うことで、用途に合わせた印象的な空間をつくることができる。

今日のデジタルコントロール技術によって、これら光りのグラフィックに対して動的変化を与えることも容易になってきていて、動く映像的表現、いわゆるモーショングラフィックスの可能性も広がってきている。

特集では、このような光りを空間デザインに融合させグラフィックに扱った例を紹介している。

Needless to say, lighting is an important element in spatial design. Utterly different environmental effects can be gained through various lighting techniques such as ambient lighting, task lighting or indirect lighting. Lighting also creates visual effects on a space with its brightness and hues. By making graphical use of these features, different spatial impressions can be produced.

With digital controlling technology, it has become easy to give dynamic changes to lighting graphics. It has expanded the application of moving images, or the so to say ability to create motion graphics.

In this feature, examples of graphical lighting integrated with spatial designs are introduced.

Lighting Graphics - I

The Monsoon Club at Kennedy Centre

Multi-purpose hall installation / Washington D.C

Designer: Serie Architects
Article: Ikunori Ara
Photography: Daniel Schwartz

（上）ステージより入り口方向見返し

(Above) Looking back at the entrance
from the stage

Feature 1: 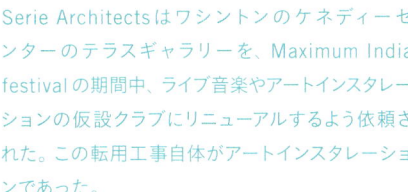 Lighting Graphics

Serie Architectsはワシントンのケネディーセンターのテラスギャラリーを、Maximum India festivalの期間中、ライブ音楽やアートインスタレーションの仮設クラブにリニューアルするよう依頼された。この転用工事自体がアートインスタレーションであった。

3次元のカーペットのようなものが吊り天井としてデザインされ、照明や音響といった必要設備もこれに組み込んでいる。

無数の糸が天井より下がり、色と光のシャワーを作る。パターンと色は伝統的なDhurriesと言うインドの織物のラグからと、Shamianaと言うムガール時代の祭典や結婚式に使用するテントよりインスパイアされたものである。

全体の大きさが60' x 28'の吊り天井は120枚のパネルに分割して制作された。各パネル（t12合板）には直径125mmの丸穴が56個開けられ、各穴から糸が垂れ下げられている。糸の色は、白、濃淡が異なる3色の青、計4色が用いられている。これら糸の配列、各パネルへの配置、吊り天井への配置はすべて一つ一つ記号が振られデジタルにパターン処理されたものである。一方、実際の制作は人の手で行われた。

20人の人手により2カ月かかって完成されたこの天井は、緩やかに波打った空飛ぶカーペットのようで、ダイナミックな印象を与える。しかし、構造的に光りのルーバー天井になっていて、重苦しさは払拭されている。

発 光 す る 伝 統 柄 の カ ー ペ ッ ト

（左）光るカーペットとしての吊り天井ディテール

(Left) Detail of the suspended ceiling as a luminous carpet

Feature 1:

Lighting Graphics

Serie Architects were invited to convert the terrace gallery at the Kennedy Centre, Washington into a temporary club for live music and art installations for the duration of the Maximum India festival. The conversion featured its own installation, a three dimensional carpet was designed as a suspended ceiling; this defined and accentuated the space whilst holding the necessary technical equipment. The million threads suspended in space created a shower of colour and light. The pattern and colour were inspired by traditional 'Dhurries' a flat Indian woven rug and also by the 'Shamiana' tent structures used for Indian feasts and weddings which dates back to the Mughal era.

Measuring 60' x 28' in total, divided into 120 plywood panels (12mm thick) suspended from the ceiling, with each panel having 56 holes of 125mm in diameter where the threads were suspended from. The location of each panel was carefully marked out mathematically and only four colours were used to create this pattern, white and 3 shades of blue, the order of threads were marked by a pixilated grid. The installation took twenty people two months to complete. As light was able to shine through the holes the result was not heavy, but a gently undulating carpet which created a dynamic atmosphere.

（左上）入り口よりステージ方向を見る
(Left above) View towards the stage from the entrance

（右）ライブ中の舞台風景
(Right) Live show on the stage

（下）ライブ中の客席風景
(Bottom) Audience during a live show

Feature 1:

Lighting Graphics

Design firm: Serie Architects
Design team: Christopher Lee, Kapil Gupta, Bolam Lee, Martin Jameson, Abdulla Yoosufali, Amit Arya, Donny Prijatna, Suril Patel and Santosh Thorat
Project team: Aditya Pawar, Anusha Bajpai, Pranav Chahande, Renu Gupta, Satish Saklani, Sunil Thukrul and Suruchi Agarwal
Installation team: Akshay Zanjale, Aniket Shivagan, Anish Sawant, Ashish Nikam, Gourav Gupta, Gouresh Hatale, Harshad Darekar, Haresh Mandavkar, Jennitta Joseph, Megha Bhatia, Mangesh Sanzgiri, Manoj Pawar, Mayur Tawade, Neeta Gurav, Ninad Masaye, Pritam Acharekar, Ramdas Gorule, Shiva Iyer, Sonam Gala, Swapnil Uttekar, Vinayak Joiel, Zainab Chauhan
Lighting consultant: AWA Lighting Designers
Supplier: N.S.Arora & Co
Carpenters: Deven Mistry, Digamber Sutar, N P Mistry, Satish Sutar, Shivaji Sutar
Painters: Anil Suryavanshi, Gorakh Jadhav, Jitendra Kadam, Prakash Suryavanshi, Sunil Jadhav
On-site Fabrication: Stockwell & J. Holdings
Total area: 350 m²
Installation: 1st ~20th Mar. 2011
Site: Kennedy Center for the Performing Arts, Washington D.C

（左）光るカーペットとしての吊り天井ディテール

(Left) Detail of the suspended ceiling as a luminous carpet

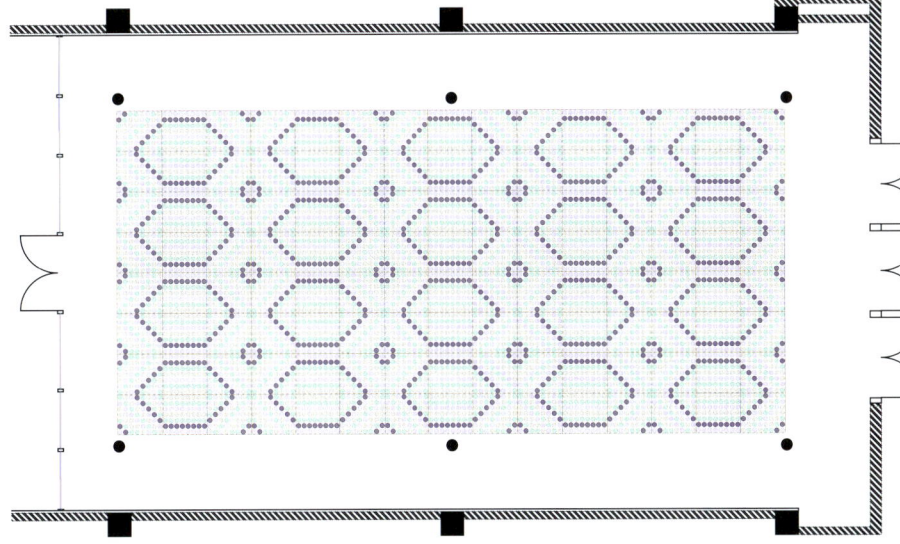

Ceiling plan

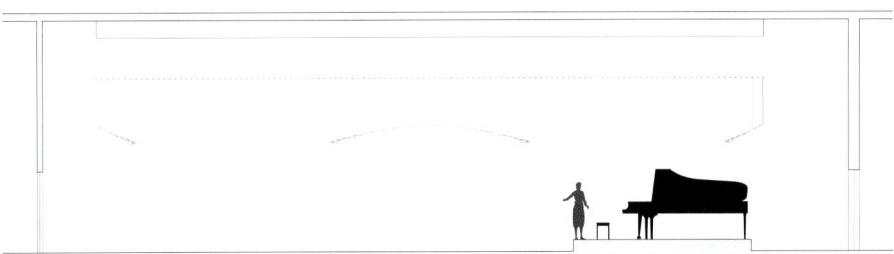

Elevation 1:200

A: Audio Tech
B: Stage

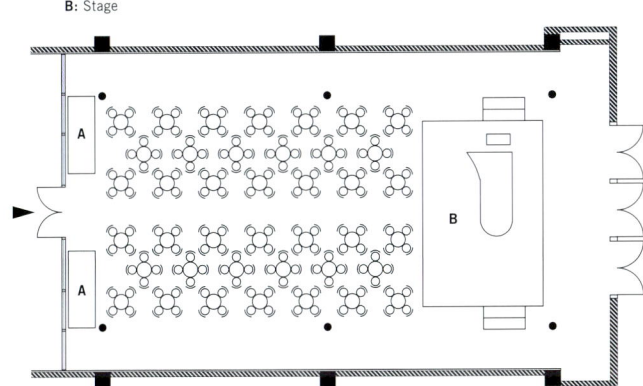

Floor plan 1:300

Construction Method-Rolling the Profiles

Tagging the panel   Direction of rotation   Rolled surface

Lighting Graphics - 2

Clyde Frazier's Wine and Dine

Restaurant and bar / New York

Designer: Morphosis
Article: Yasuhiko Taguchi
Photography: Roland Halbe

ライティングで沸き立たせた
　　　スポーツの栄光

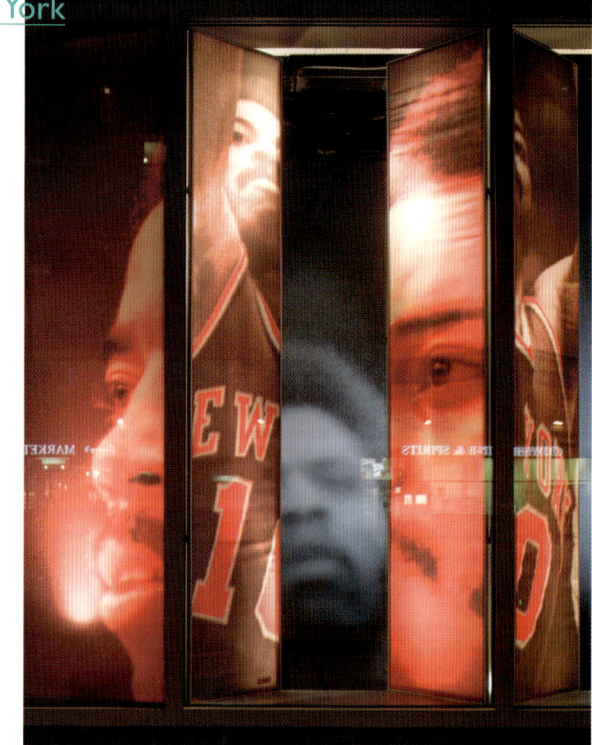

（上）外観夜景
(Above) Exterior view at night

（右）人を惑わすファサードのグラフィック
(Right) Detail of the baffling graphic
on the facade

グラフィックのある柱型を通してダイニングエリアを見る

Dining area viewed through the column with graphics

（上）メインダイニングエリア

(Above) Main dining area

（左）Scrim graphic と Liner Spectrum

(Left) View of the Scrim graphic and Liner Spectrum

Feature 1:

Lighting Graphics

元NBAニューヨークニックスのスーパースターで、バスケット以外でも影響力があり、この地の名士であるウォルト・フレイザーの店がマンハッタンにオープンした。

店は、展示会場か、インスタレーションあるいは何かのイベント会場ではないかと思われるような雰囲気をもち、伝説の人フレイザーの魅力にはまりこんでしまうような空間にデザインされた。彼の個性と常に時代の先端をいく彼のライフスタイルを生かし、店は最上級のスタイルとニックスのプレイヤーとニックスの試合のコメンテェターとしてのキャリアが表現された。

デザインは大きなスケールときっちりとした形の繰り返しによってできている。フレイザー自身のイメージを主要なインスピレーションにして、いろいろな要素を結びつけたモチーフが巧く使われ、視認性と存在感のあるポップカルチャー的スタイルとなった。外観はフレイザーの試合中の写真が都会の喧騒のなかに投影され、照明された掛け軸のようなパネルが店の存在を周辺にアピールしている。このインテリア側の壁面パネルは試合中と私生活のフレイザーを物語る内照式のグラフィクで飾られている。

彼の等身大より大きい肖像画が内照式の円柱に取り付けられ、60年と70年代のニックスの試合中の写真が4.2mの高さの壁面にコラージュされ、ダイニングエリアをパノラミックに包んでいる。

天井から吊り下がった540のメタルのウロコは店全体に流れるように取り付けられ、スペースを引き締め店全体を統一している。フレイジャーのカスタムスーツ・コレクションのファブリックをパターン化し、彫刻化したこのオブジェは店内に動きを作り、アドホックな雰囲気で顧客を包み込む。

内部の聖地的な場所には、客がフレイジャーの特色あるプレーをまねできるフリースローのコートがある。この店にはフレイジャーのオーラが満ちている。

A restaurant dedicated to former NBA New York Knicks superstar Walt "Clyde" Frazier, who has been influential off the court as well, opened in Manhattan. The place blurs the distinction between exhibition, installation, and venue, and the iconic presence of Frazier is transformed into an immersive experience. With a convergence of person and persona, it is a tribute to his trademark personality, stylish lifestyle, and his illustrious career as New York Knicks point-guard and commentator.

The design makes use of outsize scale and formal repetition. Moreover, it deftly utilizes Frazier's own image as its main inspiration and connective motif, incorporating pop-culture modalities of visibility and presence.

On the exterior, an illuminated scroll projects in-game images into the surrounding urban environment and announces the store's presence. Inside, vertical and horizontal planes provide an illustrated narrative of Frazier's life on-and-off the court.

Larger-than-life portraits of the basketball player on back-lit cylinders greet diners while a 4.2 meter-tall panoramic scrim wraps the dining area with a history of the Knicks' greatest games from the 1960s and 70s.

Some 540 metal scales hang down from the ceiling and flow through the restaurant, defining and unifying the space. Patterned from fabrics sampled from Frazier's custom suit collection, this sculptural feature directs movement and envelops the audience in an ad-hoc way.

The inner sanctum is an indoor free-throw court, inviting customers to try out the NBA Hall-of-Famer's signature moves. The entire location exudes the aura of Clyde Frazier, where he is celebrated and enshrined.

（上）ボックス席からメインダイニング方向を見る

(Above) View towards the main dining area from the box seats

Feature 1: Lighting Graphics

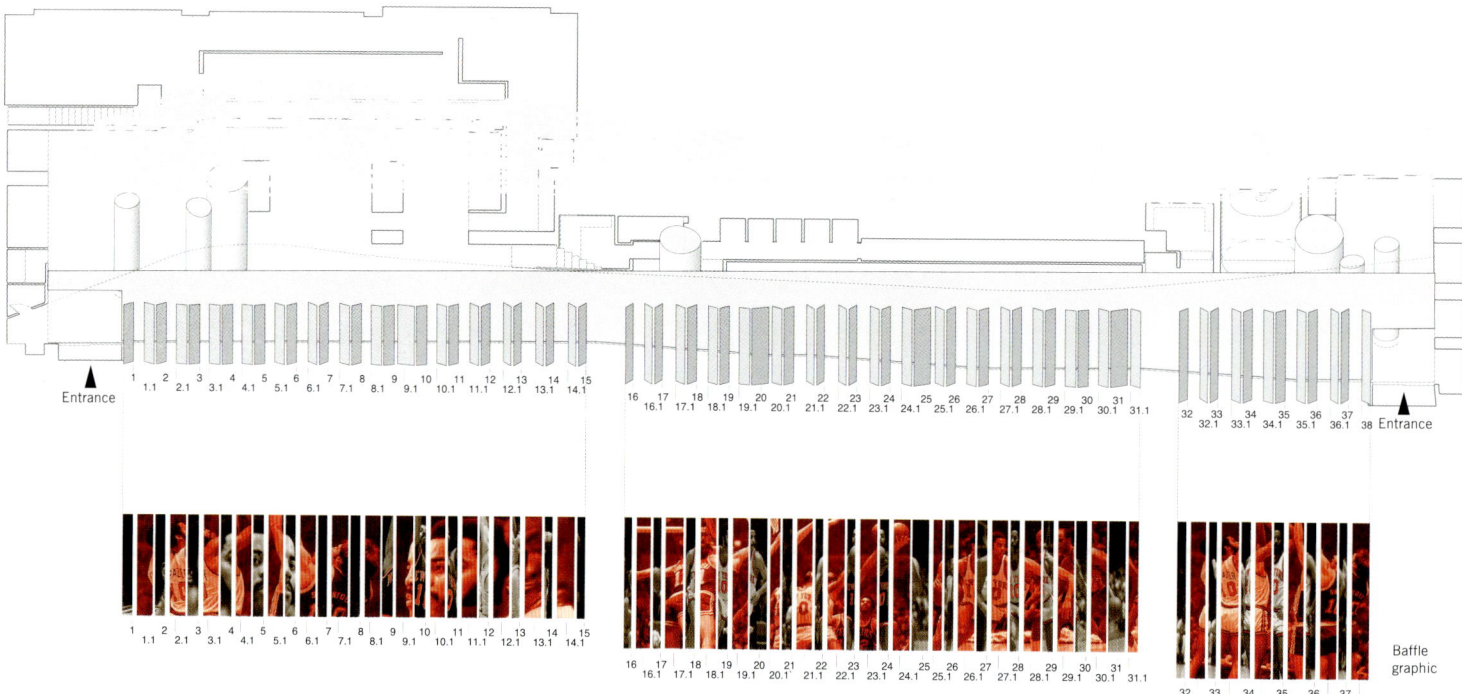

Baffle graphic

Scrim Graphic

   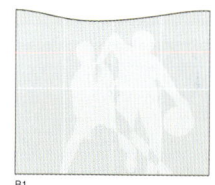   

C4　C3　B2　B1　A　C2　C1

Unfolded Column Graphic

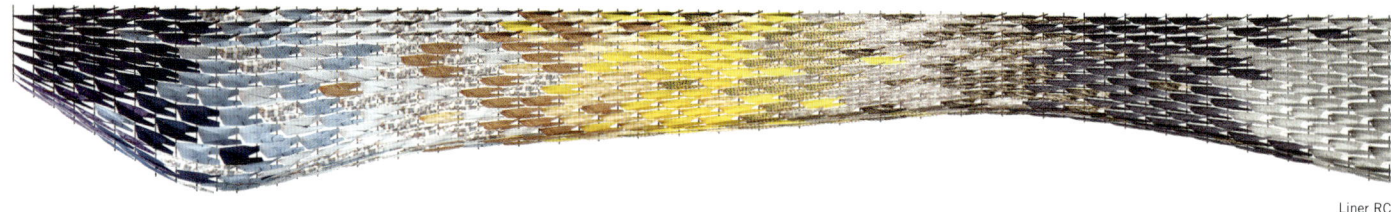

Liner RCP

Purple Viscose　Dark Blue Viscose　Blue Felt　Light Blue Corduroy　Plaid Wool　Brown Check Pattern Wool　Beige Leather　Yellow Wool　Yellow and Red/ Gingham Check Fabric　Leopard Print Fabric　Tiger Print Fabric　Black Striped Fabric　Tweed Wool

Liner Spectnum

Design firm: Morphosis
Designer: Design director; Thom Mayne, Project manager; Ung-Joo Scott Lee
Project designer: Natalia Traverso Caruana, Suzanne Tanascaux, Satoru Sugihara
Project team: Nicholas Shrier, Alayne Kaethler,

Project assistants: Nicholas Fayad, Sunkyu Koh, Jeff Gilway, Pavio Kryvozub, Kyung-Eun Lee
Project management/Owner's Representative: Linda Clous
Director of Facilities and Project management: ARK Restaurants

Consultant:
Structural engineer- Gerard Santora, P.E., Santora Engineering, Prego, P.E. Consulting Engineers
Acoustic- Shen Milsom Wilke, Kitchen-Jacobs / Doland
Lighting- Tillotson Design Associates, Environmental graphics- Morphosis Architects
2D Graphics- Patricia Spencer Design

Total area: 930m²
Contractor: T. Higgins Construction Corporation Inc.
Client: ARK Restaurants
Completion: May 2012
Main materials: Glass, metal, Resin Panels, Cement, Wood
Site: 485 10th Ave New York, NY

Feature 1:　　　　　　　　　　　　　　　　　　Lighting Graphics

Designer: Muti Randolph
Article: Yasuhiko Taguchi　　　　Lighting Graphics - 3
Photography: Leonardo Finotti

D.Edge 2.0

Culb / São Paulo

ラインライトの皮膜で
空間を包む

2階クラブ。窓側ボックス席を見る

2nd floor club. View towards the box
seats along the window

オリジナルのD-エッジが2003年にサンパウロにオープンした時、LEDテクノロジーとカスタム・ソフトウェアの使用で音と光のシステムを統合した最初のクラブとして話題になったが、クラブ以上に、そこは音と光のインスタレーションの場であった。聴くだけではなく、音楽を見たり感じたりする装置であったのだ。オープンして7年が経過し、今では世界の著名なDJがこぞって出演する有名なエレクトロニック・ミュージック・クラブになった。
今回オーナーは隣接している家を購入しクラブを拡張するに当たって、オリジナルと同じインパクトのあるクラブで、世界で最も心地よいオープンな

喫煙所を加え、同じく心地よいトイレの数を多くし、入場窓口を増やし、身障者用エレベーターを設置し、ニーマイヤー設計のラテンアメリカ記念公園の眺望を取り入れた開放感のある屋上テラスを加えるよう求めた。
空間にインパクトを作る三つの要素が考えられた。1番目の要素は2階で、天井、壁、バー、DJブースを結ぶLEDが木のストライプの床に埋められ、新しいダンスフロアーが作られた。特別に作られたソフトウェアで音楽を全体にシンクロさせ、ライブアニメーションを展示する3D回路の光のネットワークが作られた。壁の一つは他から光を反射す

る大きな鏡であるが、実は部分的に視界を妨げるLEDが埋め込まれたライトボックスで、20mの窓をカバーしている鏡である。
2番目の要素は3階にあるラウンジで、ランダムな回転角度に配列された四つの異なった濃淡の木のブロックで構成されている。ここでは、あたかも音楽が小さな地震のように建物が揺れ、音楽が感じられる心地の良い場所である。
3番目の要素は内部と外部から光を発し、内部に光の動きを見せる波形のアルミボックスの新しいファサードである。
既存のクラブとは1階の通路で結ばれた。

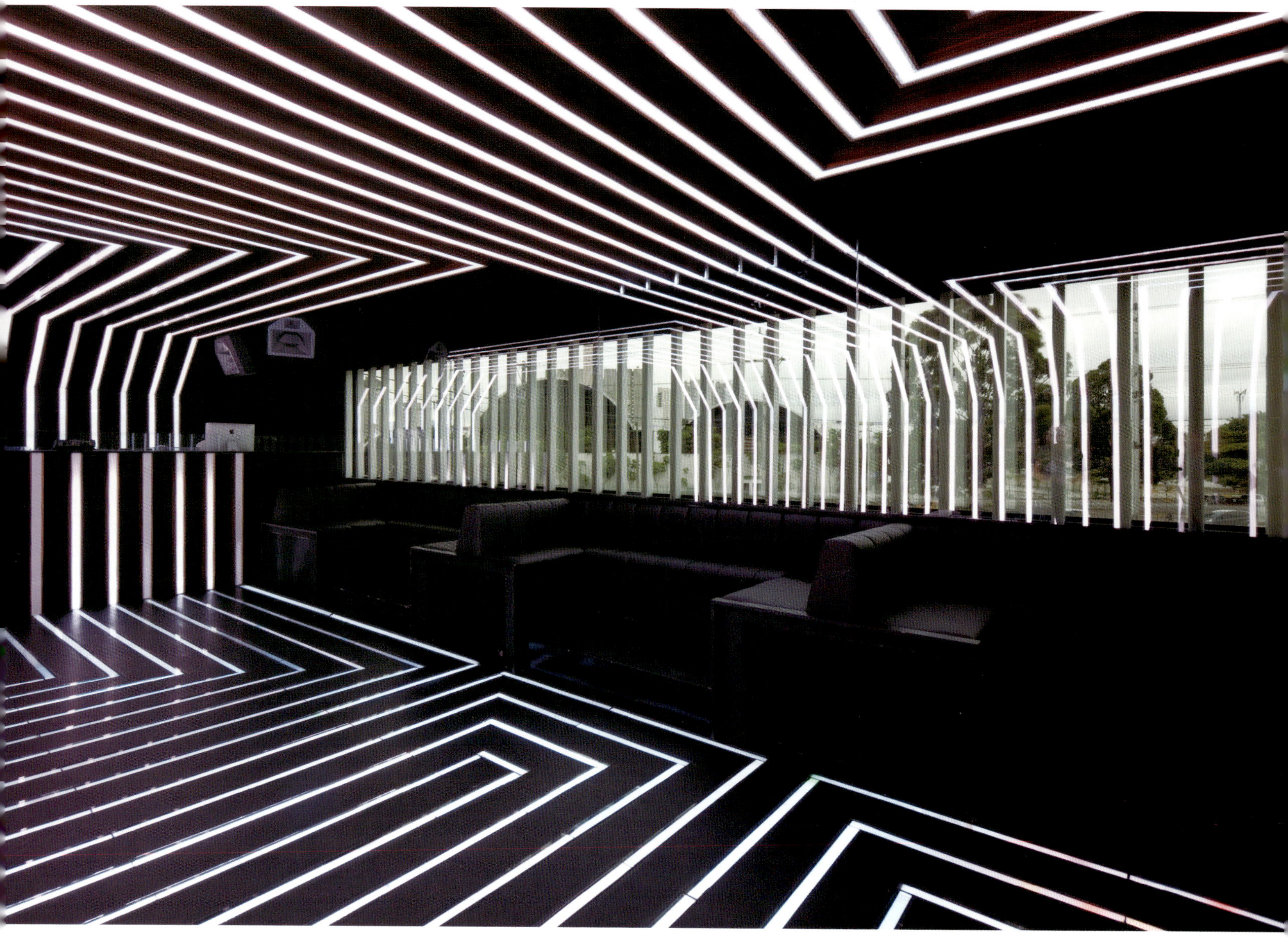

（上）2階クラブ。エレベータホールより
見る

(Above) 2nd floor club. Viewed from the
elevator hall

（左）2階クラブ。ラインライトはデジタル
コントロールされている

(Left) 2nd floor club. Digitally controlled line light

Feature 1:

Lighting Graphics

（右・下）3階ラウンジ

(Right, Bottom) 3rd floor lounge

（右・下）3階ラウンジ

(Right, Bottom) 3rd floor lounge

Feature 1:

Lighting Graphics

（左上）1階。レセプションフロア
(Left above) 1st floor. Reception floor

（右上）屋上の円筒形トイレ
(Right above) Cylindrical W.C. on the rooftop

（左）2003年にオープンした既存のクラブ
(Left) Club opened in 2003

When the original D-Edge opened its doors in 2003 in Sao Paulo, Brazil, it became the talk of the town as the first club to integrate sound and light systems with the use of LED technology and custom software. More than a club, it is a sound and light installation, a place where people not only hear, but also see and feel the music. In the seven years after its opening, it has become a prestigious electronic music club where the biggest DJs from around the world have played.

When the owner purchased the house next door and commissioned an expansion, the requirements included more comfort, an open smoking area, and the same impact as the original one. The comfort was addressed with more restrooms, a new reception with multiple cash registers, an elevator for the disabled, and a wide-open terrace with a view to Niemeyer's Memorial da America Latina across the street.

For impact, the designer focused on three elements. The first was a new dance floor composed of protruded wood strips embedded with LEDs that connect the ceiling, one of the walls, the bar, and the DJ booth. Forming a network of light lines, custom software and three-dimensional circuitry can display real-time animation in synch with the music. One of the walls is a large mirror that reflects light; in fact, it is actually a false mirror that covers a 20 meter window with embedded LED light boxes that partially obstruct the view.

The second impact feature is the third floor lounge, which includes interceding blocks of four different shades of wood, placed in random rotation angles. The result is as if the music caused a small earthquake and shook the building, yet, the area is a comfortable place to listen to the smooth music.

The third element of impact is the new façade, which is a corrugated aluminum box with a window that reveals some of the light action inside. Meanwhile, a first floor corridor connects the expansion to the existing club.

Feature 1:   Lighting Graphics

Designer: Muti Randolph
Colabrators: Marcelo Pontes, Eduardo Chalabi, Paula Zemel
Total area: 800m²
Client: Renato Ratier
Completion: Nov. 2010
Main materials: Resin floor, wood, plexiglas, glass, LED, corrugated aluminum
Site: Alameda Olga 170, São Paulo

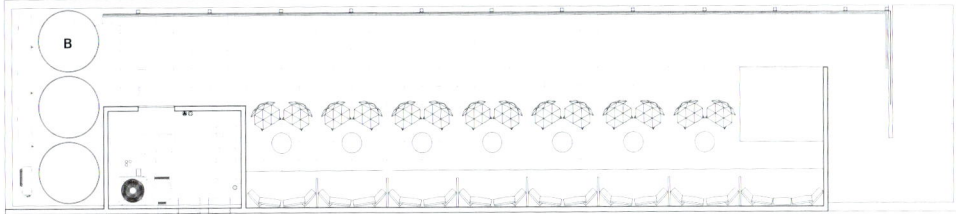

Roof top plan

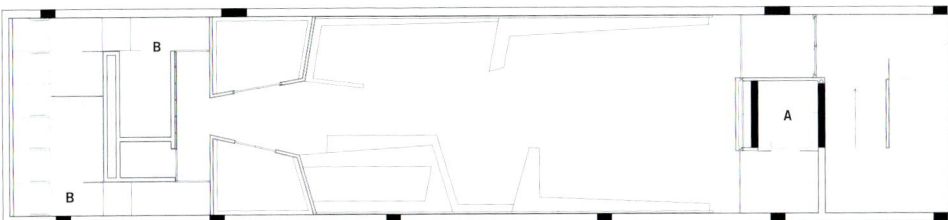

3rd floor plan

2nd floor plan 1:200

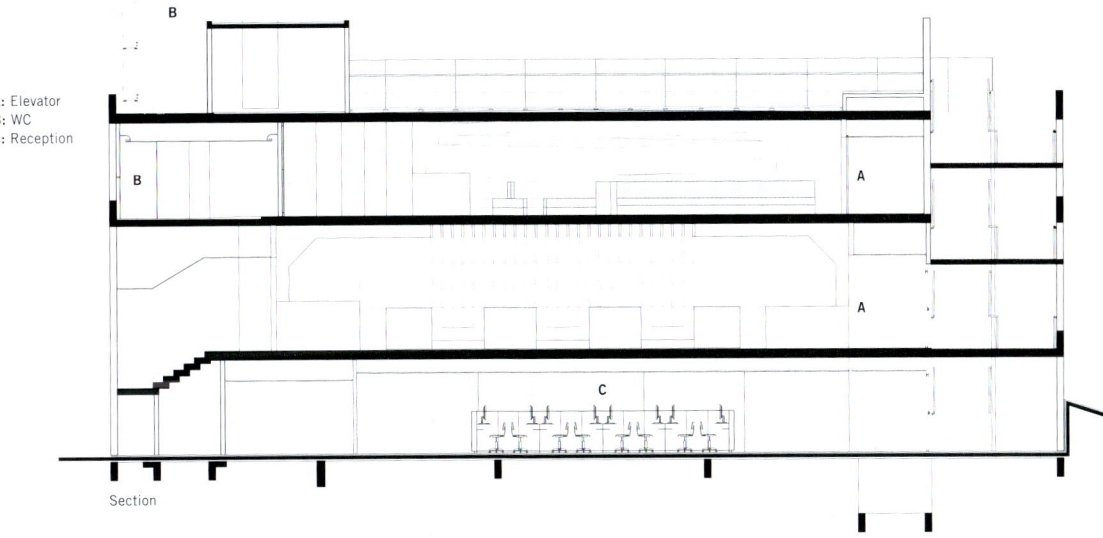

A: Elevator
B: WC
C: Reception

Section

（左下）ファサード夜景

(Left bottom) Exterior view at night

（右下）屋上客席

(Right) Rooftop seats

映像で結ばれたペアショップ

Designer: March Studio
Article: Ikunori Ara
Photography: Rodney Eggleston (March Studio)

Bondi Junction

（上）ショーウインドーをかねたスチール
ドアは夜は閉まる

(Above) Perforated steel door closed
at night

（中）ドアはスチールの軸柱で回転する

(Middle) Door revolving on a steel pivot

（下）営業中はドアは開け放たれる

(Bottom) Doors kept open in business
hours

（右上）店内入り口右側より見る

(Right above) Store viewed from the
entrance right side

Lighting Graphics - 4

Aesop Twins;
Aesop Westfield Bondi Junction and
Aesop Westfield City Centre

Skincare shop / Sydney

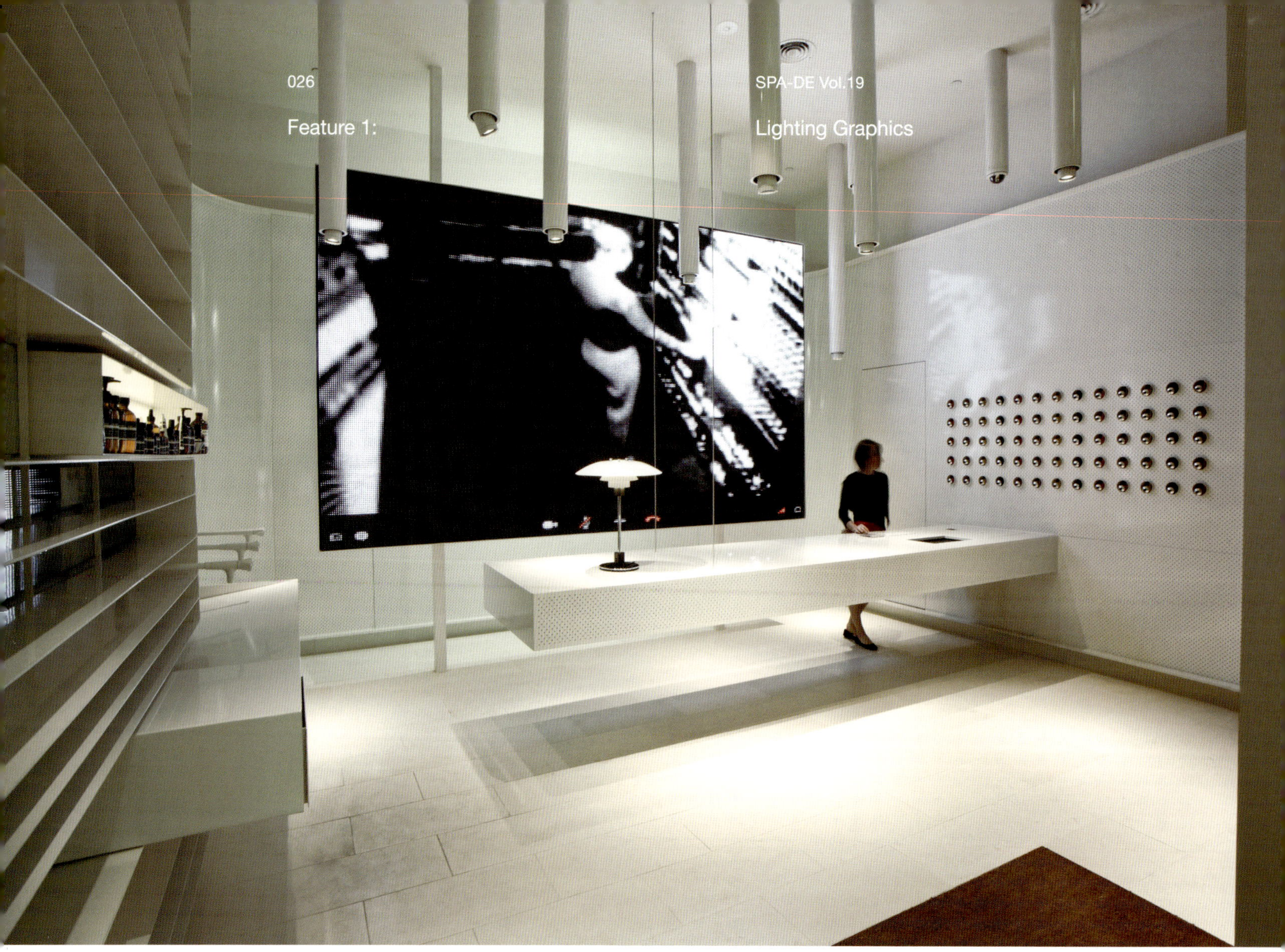

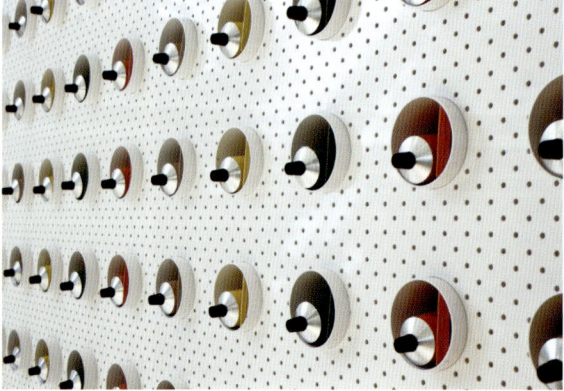

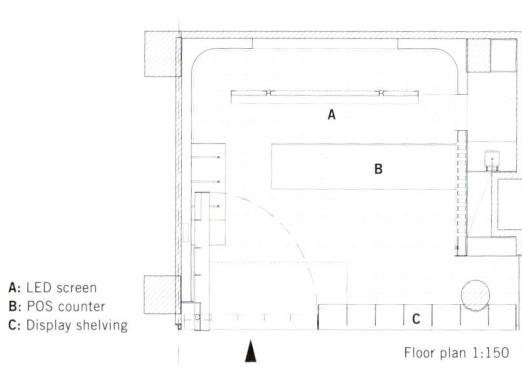

（左）円筒形のディスプレイボックス

(Left) Cylindrical display boxes

（上）入り口より店内を見る

(Above) right side of the entrance

A
B
C

A: LED screen
B: POS counter
C: Display shelving

Floor plan 1:150

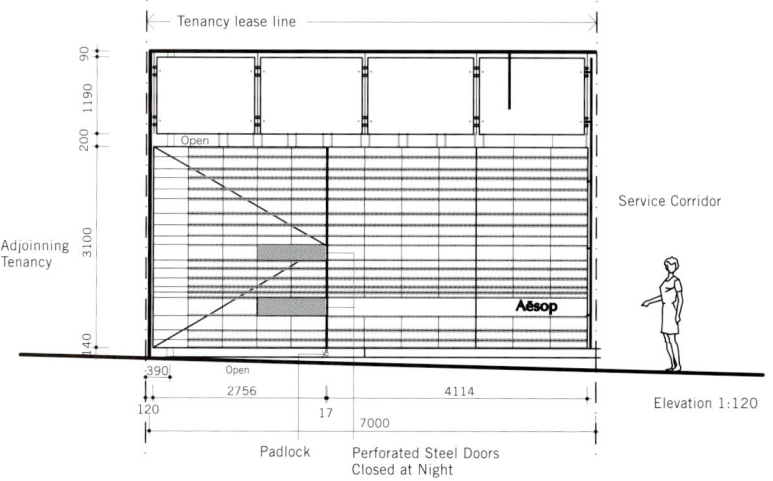

Tenancy lease line
90
1190
200
3100
140
Open
Adjoinning Tenancy
Service Corridor
Aēsop
390
Open
2756
4114
120
17
7000
Padlock
Perforated Steel Doors Closed at Night

Elevation 1:120

Feature 1:

Lighting Graphics

City
Centre

Designer: March Studio
Project team: Rodney Eggleston, Julian Canterbury, Anne-Laure Cavigneaux
Client: Aesop Pty Ltd.
Completion: Mar. 2012
Total area: Bondi Junction 31.5m², City Centre 22m²
Contractor: CBD Contracting Pty Ltd
Main Material: Clear glass, Pegboard, Steel (Bondi Junction; Powder coated, City Centre; Row), LED screen
Site:
Aesop Westfield Bondi Junction; Shop 3018, Westfield Bondi Junction, Bondi Junction, Sydney
Aesop Westfield City Centre; Shop 74007, Level 4, Westfield Sydney City, Sydney

（右）入り口より店内左側を見る

(Right) Left side of the store viewed from the entrance

（下）入り口方向見返し。半開きのドアがミラー壁に映っている

(Bottom) Looking back at the entrance. Semi-opened door reflected on the mirror wall

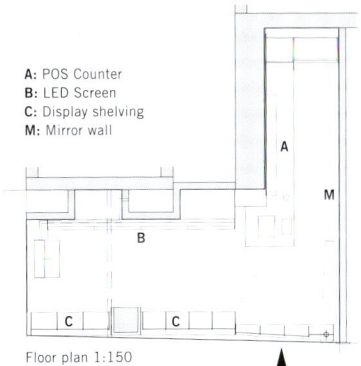

A: POS Counter
B: LED Screen
C: Display shelving
M: Mirror wall

Floor plan 1:150

オーストラリア発祥のスキンケアブランド、イソップはすでに世界に45の路面店を持ち、なお増殖中である。店舗展開の特徴としてこれまで一つとして同じデザインの店がないということが挙げられる。オーストラリアのショップデザインは1号店からMarch Studioが担当してきたが、今回は二つの店を初めてペアのショップとして同時にデザインした。March studioが採用したデザイン手法は「共通点」と「対比点」を際立たせて採り入れるというものであった。共通点の一つはドアとして開閉する大きなディスプレイ棚で、閉店後はショッピングモールに対してショーウインドーの機能を果たす。対比点の一つはクリーム色と黒という正反対のカラースキーム。

そして、お互いのインテリアを映し出す大きなビデオスクリーンがカウンターバックに配され、映像面で「双子性」が強調されている。

Australian skincare brand Aesop has 45 shops all over the world with even more planned. March Studio designed the very first store and has now completed the Twin Aesop stores in Sydney, where for the first time 2 stores have almost the same design, all the other stores being distinctly different. For the Twin Aesop design there are similarities and also opposites to make them unique, yet the same. Both shops have entrance doors that are actually huge display shelves, which can be swung back against the wall and on closing products are displayed to passersby in the mall. One store is predominantly cream the other is opposing black. The shops are also linked by a video projection of the other twin's activities on large LED video screens behind the cash desk in each store. Thus like twins they are permanently connected.

Feature 1:

ＲＧＢの照射で
柄が変化する壁紙

Lighting Graphics - 5

RGB

Wallcovering Exhibition / London

Designer: Carnovsky
Article: Ikunori Ara
Photography: Jeff Metal

Carnovsky は、ミラノのアーティスト兼デザイナーの Francesco Rugi と Silvia Quintanilla の事務所である。彼らが製作したアートワークは RGB のテクニックを使用したもので、これは単色による3個のイメージを重ね合わせた印刷である。そのため赤、緑、青の光を当てると、その内の一つのイメージしか見えないが、白色光の下では綺麗な絵がそっくりそのまま重なって見えることになる。
ロンドンの DreamBags-JaguarShoes での新作

壁紙のエキジビションでは、豊富な植物と動物のジャングルがテーマで行なわれた。内部のスペースは、白地と黒地の二つに分けられ、昼夜を表している。特に黒地の方は、ネガティブに見えるのが面白い。このエキジビションは額縁に入った絵を展示したのではなく、床から天井までフルハイトのため、常に変化する色やパターンを体感できる。なお、ここは80年代、靴屋とバッグ屋だったが、店名を残したまま現在はカフェバー営業をしている。

（左上）入り口より展示会場左手を見る
（右上）展示会場左手奥より見る
(Left above) Exhibition area viewed from the entrance
(Right above) Exhibition area viewed from the inner left side

Feature 1:   Lighting Graphics

Carnovsky is a Milan based artist/designer duo Francesco Rugi and Silvia Quintanilla. They create beautiful artworks using the RGB technique, which consists of three images printed in a single primary colour overlaid to form a multi-layered print. Placing red, green or blue light onto the work conceals all but one of the images while white light reveals the beautiful picture in its entirety.

They had an exhibition at DreamBags-JaguarShoes, a place that was previously two shops that were converted into one bar, exhibition space and art sales but keeping the original names. New wallpapers were created with a jungle theme of abundant vegetation and creatures. The interior space was divided into two halves with the paper having white background in one part and black in another, as if day and night. Following the same RGB principle but inverted, on black the world appears in negative. This exhibition was not just a picture it was a floor to ceiling ever changing magical experience.

Designer: Carnovsky
Design team: Francesco Rugi and Silvia Quintanilla
Period: 28th Jul.–30th Oct. 2011
Main materials: Paper
Exhibition location: DreamBags-Jaguar-Shoes, 32-34 Kingsland Road, Shoreditch, London

（右）RGBライトの切り替えによって壁紙のパターンが変化する

(Right) Wall paper pattern varies by switching the RGB lighting

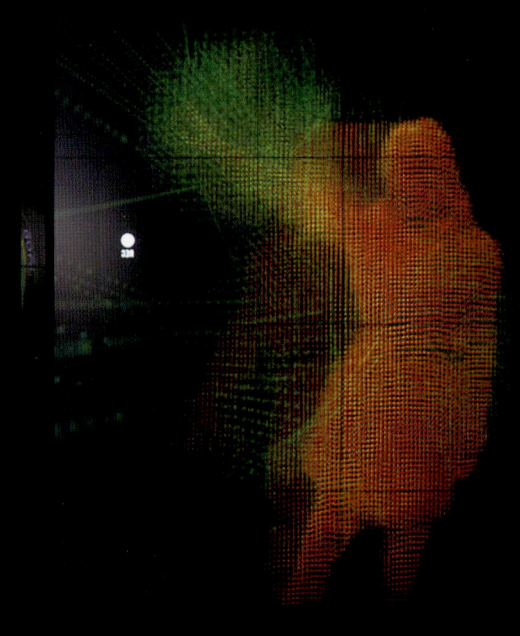

Lighting Graphics - 6

NIKE + Fuelstation at Boxpark

Concept Store / London

インタラクティブな
モーショングラフィックス

Designer: NIKE Brand Design Europe
Article: Ikunori Ara
Photography: Julian Abrams (Except Boxpark Exterior)

NIKEのコンセプトショップが、東ロンドンのPop-up Boxpark モールに作られた。このモールは4年間期間限定のテンポラリーなもので、海運用コンテナを数個並べただけという大胆な発想の下で作られた。

デザインはハウスデザイナーチームNike brand design teamが行ない、彼らによるNIKEの1号店からの積み重ねを踏まえながら、未来的デザインを入れ込んだものとした。1階のデザインはNIKEの技術を顧客へ伝えるように、材料やデジタルサービスや視覚的インタラクションを利用できることであった。入口近くの人の動きをカメラが追い、壁面の色がそれに連動して赤から緑へと変わる。またNike fuel podの中心ともいえる「モーション

センシティブLEDウオールI」では顧客の動きを記録し、何千ものピクセルによってシルエット化している。このデータは希望する顧客のPCに送信することもできる。オリジナル1号店で使用していたブリーチ木材の壁面仕上げも採用したが、当時はペイントで描かれていた番号は、ここではLCD (Liquid Cristal Display) によって描かれている。

2階は顧客がプロダクトと遊べる空間である。商品を展示した22mの棚に、靴底をデジタル処理するNIKEのデザインサービスを利用できるiMacを収納した特注ガラステーブルなどがある。また顧客の生理学的スポーツチェックをする部屋もある。ここで人びとは今までにない新しい買い物体験ができる。

（上）Nike fuel pod のモーションセンシティブLEDウオール

(Above) Motion sensing LED screen wall at the Nike fuel pod

（下）Boxparkモールの外観

(Bottom) Exterior view of Boxpark Mall

Feature 1:   Lighting Graphics

Design Firm: Nike Brand Design Europe
Design Team: Nick Parkinson, Marjolijn
van Puffelen, Gary Horton
Client: NIKE
Area: 200m²
Open: Feb. 2012
Contractor: Millington Associates
Main Materials: Bleacher wood,
Concrete, Glass, Digital technology
Site: Boxpark, 2-4 Bethanal Green Road,
London, E1 6GY

Nike has opened a concept store, the Nike+Fuel Station in East London. Situated in the pop-up Boxpark Mall, which is an innovation itself as the mall is made from shipping containers and will only be open for four years.

Designed by the in house Nike brand design team the store mixes futuristic interior design with features inspired from the first ever Nike store. The design of the ground floor is about bringing Nike technology to customers through the use of material, digital services and visual interaction. On entering movement is tracked by a camera, which turns the wall from red to green. There is also the Nike fuel pod with its motion sensitive LED wall on which customer's movement is recorded as a silhouette made of thousands of pixels that can be sent to the customers' own computer. As in the original store the fuel station features the iconic shaped bleacher wooden wall given a modern twist with embedded LCD counting numbers replacing the hand painted digits on the original.

The area upstairs is for customising and letting consumers have fun with products, the design reflects this. A main feature is a 22m long shelf to showcase products; there are bespoke glass tables with drop down imacs for utilising the Nike design service, a digitized treadmill and even a physio room.

In this store the shopping experience is redefined.

（上上）インタラクティブなタッチスクリーン壁

(Above above) Interactive 92" touch screen wall

（上）2階の顧客がプロダクトと遊べる空間

(Above) Area on the 2nd floor where customers can play with products

Feature 1:   Lighting Graphics

Lighting Graphics - 7

Mi- Sha

Temporary restaurant / Milano

Designer: Simone Micheli
Article: Masaatsu Fukazawa
Potography: Jurgen Eheim

この実験的映像レストランは2011年4月、ミラノ家具サロンの期間に合わせて6日間だけオープンした。ドゥオモ広場に面しミラノの中心とも言えるガレリアの中にあるホテルSeven Stars Galleriaの「王の間」という天井高7mのクラッシックな広間を使ってのインスタレーションである。
企画コンセプトはこのホテル経営者のA. Rossoと建築家S. Micheliが立案した。2010年のエキスポ上海から、2015年のエキスポミラノ～テーマ；「地球を養う、生活のためのエネルギー」食料問題～への繋ぎの催しとしており、ミラノの伝統的料理と中華料理をフュージョンした料理がサービスされた。大広間の空間にミラノと現代中国の都市風景や時代の情景が映し出された。ちなみにMi-ShaはMilano-Shanghaiの略。
これらの映像は、この空間の各所に置かれた八つの白いキューブ（MDF製、60cm立方）からプロジェクションされたもので、キューブには大小さまざまな大きさの丸い穴が開けられている。一つは投影口、他は放熱口でこれ自体がオブジェになっている。既存のクラシカルな壁面上に投影されたイメージは次々に変化し、多様な雰囲気をかもし出す。中央2カ所ある天井から吊られたこれまたクラッシックなシャンデリアは、白い半透明のカーテンで巻かれ空間を現代的に演出している。その下に配置された椅子やテーブルのデザインは雑多だが色は白で統一している。椅子の背に謎めいたマークとして黒い手のひらがプリントされている。伝統と革新、過去と未来、その形と多様性、それらをひっくるめ人々をその空間に投げ込む実験的な空間と言える。

（左上）会期中設けられたレセプションデスク

(Left above) Reception desk installed during the event

（上）ビットリオ・エマニュエル2世大広間の中央付近より見る

(Above) View from the central part of Sala Vittorio Emannele II

クラシックインテリアと
プロジェクション映像の
コラボレーション

Designer: Simone Micheli
Concept: Alessandro Rosso and Simone
Micheli
Client: Alessandro Rosso Group
Internal finishes:
Adrenalina, Axia contract division,
Chelini, Cyrus Company, Désirée,
Doimo Contract, DoimOffice, Euromobil,
Fiandre Architectural Surfaces,
Myyour, Tao, Zonca

Technical partner:
Associazione Italiana Maggiordomi,
Pointex,
RaDa collezioni- WKM factory, Sign
System
Period: Apr. 12-17 2011
Site: Galleria V. Emanuele II 11-12,
Milano

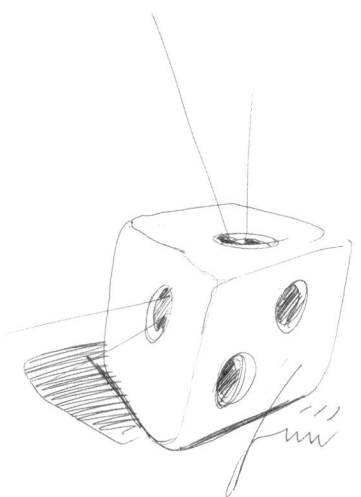

（上）ラウンジ側から見る

(Above) View from the lounge

（左）広間には8箇所にプロジェクターボックスが置かれている

(Left) Projector boxes laid at eight places in the Sala

（左下）プロジェクターボックスのスケッチ

(Left above) Sketch of the projecter box

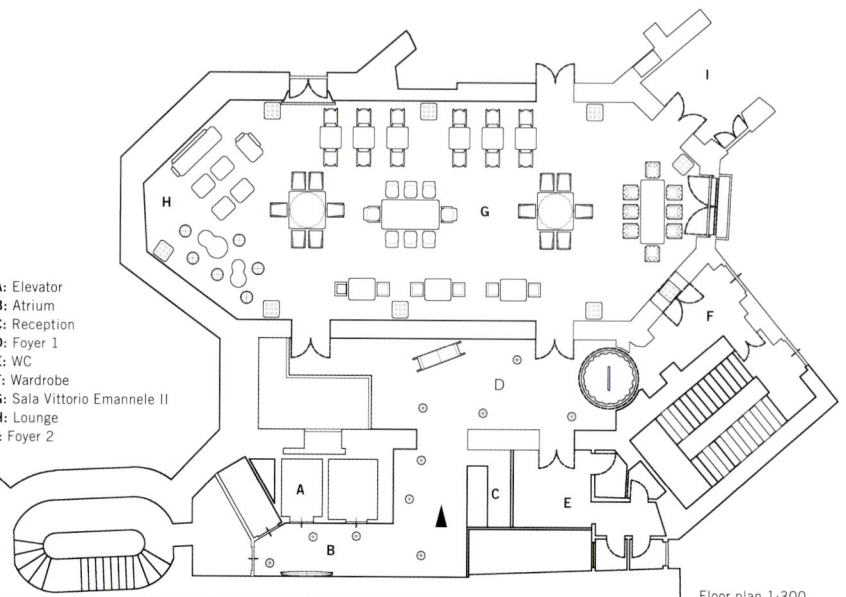

A: Elevator
B: Atrium
C: Reception
D: Foyer 1
E: WC
F: Wardrobe
G: Sala Vittorio Emannele II
H: Lounge
I: Foyer 2

Floor plan 1:300

Feature 1:   Lighting Graphics

（上）ラウンジまわり

(Above) Around the lounge

This experimental restaurant using projected imagery was open only for 6 days during the FuoriSalone week in Milan (April 12-17, 2011). It was an installation using the King's Hall with the 7 meter-high ceiling in the Seven Stars Galleria hotel in the heart of Milan.

The owner of the hotel, A. Rosso and architect S. Micheli conceived the idea to link the Expo in Shanghai in 2010 and Expo in Milan to be held in 2015 under the theme of food "Feed the Planet, Energy for Life." Traditional dishes in Milan combined with Chinese cuisine were served.

On the classical walls, cityscapes of Milan and cities in present-day China were projected one after another, and created changing atmospheres. These images were pro-jected from the eight white cubes (made of medium-density fiberboards of 60 cubic m.) installed at different places in the hall. Each cube has large and small holes, one of which is for projection and the rest for heat release. These cubes functioned also as interior objects.

The two classic chandeliers hanging from the ceiling were covered with translucent curtains to look like modern interior objects. The tables and chairs were varied in design but were unified with white. Black mysterious hand marks are printed on the backrest of chairs. It is an experimental space intended to allure people into the mixture of tradition and innovation, unity and diversity, and the past and the future.

Feature 1:　　　　　　　　　　　　　Lighting Graphics

Designer: Dan Brunn architect
Article: Yasuhiko Taguchi
Photography: Taiyo Watanabe

Lighting Graphics - 8

Yojisan Sushi

Temporary restaurant / Milano

光りで表現された
竹林のメタファー

Design firm: Dan Brunn architect
Designer: Dan Brunn
Consultant:
Graphics and Logo- Julie Priceman of 6 Degrees LA
Audio Video- Jon Komen of Swayd Systems
Exterior Sign- Ruben Cielak of Tako Tyko
Total area: 154m² / 52 Seats

Contractor: Ken Nishio of Tokyo Construction, Inc.
Client: Giacomino Drago
Completion: Apr. 2012
Total budget: $400,000
Main materials: Tile, Stone, wood, Cloth, Concrete, Steel
Site: 260 N. Beverly Dr., Beverly Hills, Los Angeles

ロサンゼルスでも高級店がたち並ぶノースビバリードライブにオープンしたスシレストラン。店は周囲の型にはまらず。日本の文化、ライフスタイル、材料からヒントを得たものをデザイン要素として用い、視覚的インパクトを街並に与えている。

ファサードは杉板の竪羽目貼り。入口の導入部天井では植物が逆さまに吊り下がり、照明で照らされ、日本の森を思わせるようにデザインされた。レセプションデスクの後方には内部が赤いウルシの重箱を逆にしたような大きな照明ボックスが付けられ温かみと華やかさを出している。

両側の壁はそれぞれ異なった意図でデザインされている。左側の既存のレンガ壁は音響効果と柔らかさを出すために半透明のカーテンが付けられている。反対側の壁はランダムに傾斜した照明の帯が、竹林を思わせるようにアレンジされている。この照明は特別に作られた布とプラスチックで構成されている。主動線はこの壁に沿っていて、内照式壁は"ネガの竹林"を散歩する楽しさを演出している。

（左上）店内右側壁面を入り口左側より見る
(Left above) Right side wall viewed from the entrance left side

（右上）ファサード
(Right above) Facade

（右下）入り口より店内を見る
(Right bottom) Restaurant viewed from the entrance

Opening in North Beverly Drive in Los Angeles, California and flanked by high-end storefronts is a new Japanese restaurant. Instead of resorting to existing Beverly Hills clichés, the designer introduces a simple, yet substantial visual impact to the neighborhood, inspired by traditional Japanese culture, lifestyle, and materials.

The façade composed of vertical cedar planks beckons diners. At the entrance, they walk under a floating carpet of plants hanging down from the ceiling and lit from above; the design invokes a Japanese forest dreamscape. Beyond the host desk, the ceiling makes way for two giant, inverted bento boxes of a red finish that provide a warm, emanating glow to the interior.

Along the perimeter, the two walls have a unique purpose. The existing brick wall is a warm material seen through a

sheer curtain that softens the space and acts as an acoustic buffer. Opposite this wall is an array of angled light coves evoking dynamic bamboo shoots. Each light strand is clad with a custom cloth and plastic composite. This wall functions as the main circulation artery and creates a playful sensation of traversing through a field of illuminated stalks by playing with negative space.

（上）ホストカウンターよりテーブル席を見る

(Above) Dining area viewed from the host counter

（下）店内奥スシカウンター前より入り口方向見返し

(Bottom) Looking back at the entrance from the inner side sushi counter

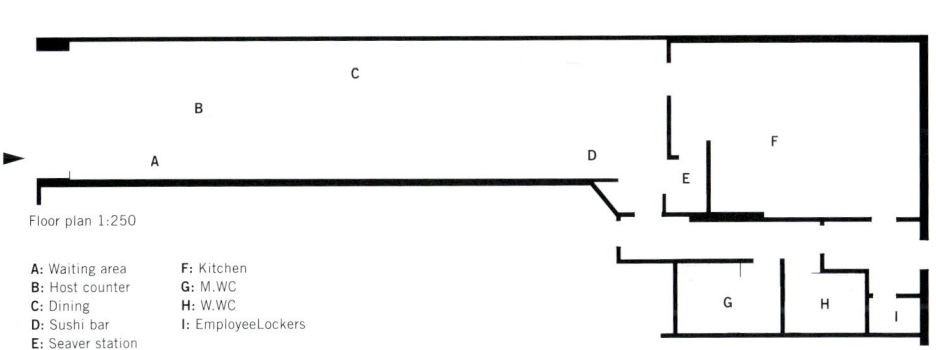

Floor plan 1:250

A: Waiting area
B: Host counter
C: Dining
D: Sushi bar
E: Seaver station
F: Kitchen
G: M.WC
H: W.WC
I: EmployeeLockers

Feature 2

Elaborately Designed Food Shops

特集 2

ハイデザイン・フードショップ

空間デザインと一体になって食の豊かさや楽しさを情報発信できるような「食物販」の店。現代において「食」や「味」は美学に近いクリエイティブな精神を求められている。料理で器や盛りつけが大切なように、「食物販」では空間デザインが美味しさを主張する手段として重要になってきている。

ワイン、パン、チョコレート、オリーブオイル、ヨーグルト、コーヒーなどを扱う世界の最新デザインの店を紹介。

Beautifully designed food shops present the richness of food products and the pleasure of eating. Today, nearly aesthetic creativity is required to express food and flavor. Just as serving dishes and ways to dish up are important in cooking, spatial design is becoming essential for food shops as a means to present the deliciousness of the merchandise.
Food shops with cutting edge designs selling wine, bread, chocolate, olive oil, yogurt, coffee, etc., are presented here.

Corné
1932

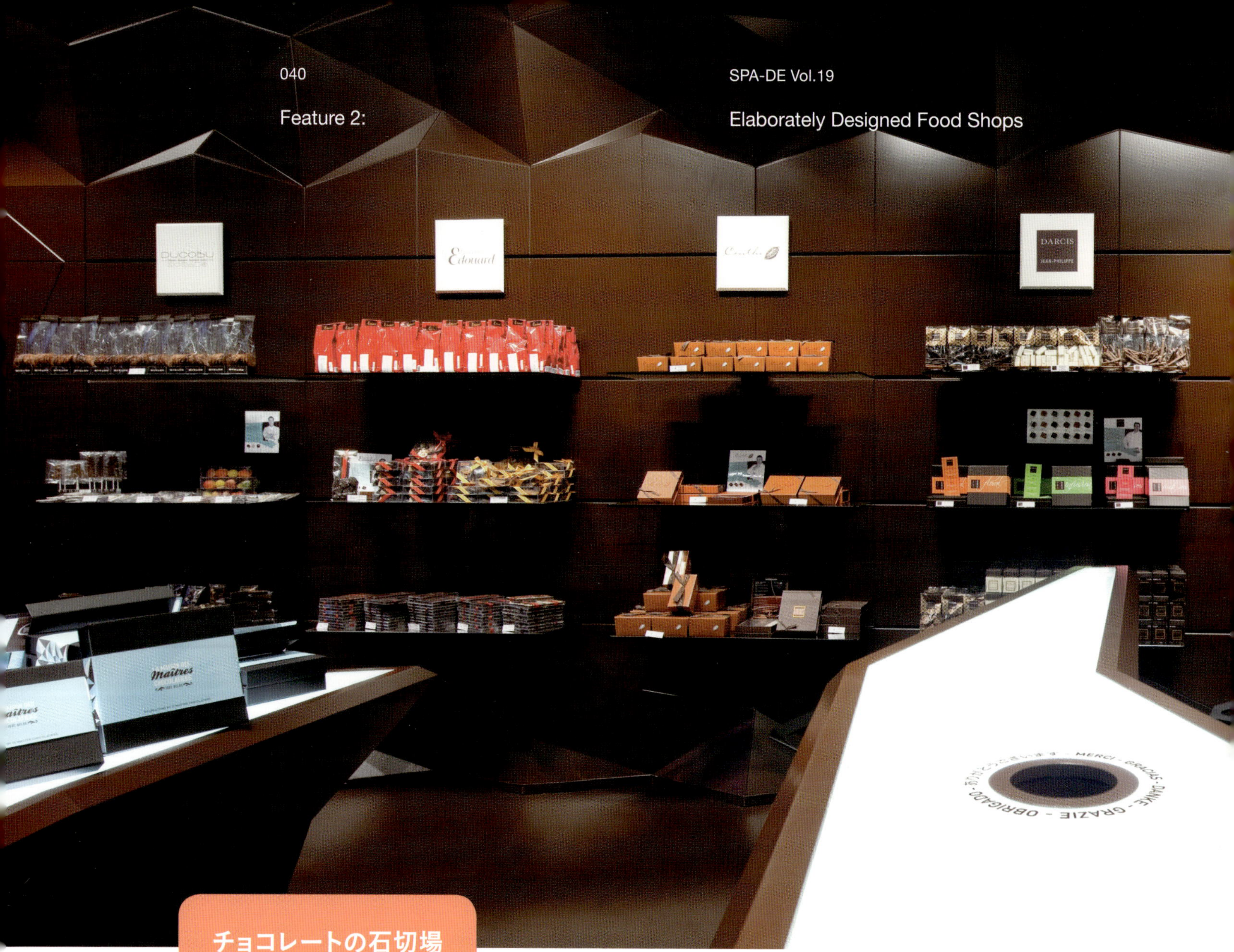

チョコレートの石切場

（下）外観夕景
(Bottom) Twilight view of the facade

Elaborately Designed Food Shops - 1

La Maison des Maîtres Chocolatiers

Chocolate shop / Brussels

Designer: Minale Design Strategy
Article: Yasuhiko Taguchi
Photography: Olivier Seignette

（左）店内左側を見る
(Left) View of the left side in the store

（下）店内右側を見る
(Bottom) View of the right side in the store

Feature 2: Elaborately Designed Food Shops

L'ACADÉMIE
DES MAÎTRES

EXIGENCE

Savoir-faire

PASSION

Découvertes

ATELIER

TRADITION

ベルギー国際チョコレート協界は、チョコレート職人のための場を作ることによってベルギー・チョコレートをプロモートするユニークなショップを求めた。コンセプトは、感動するような空間、試食ができ、イベントの場としてブランドの情報発信の拠点になり、一般の人々にベルギー・チョコレートを知ってもらうショーケース、というものであった。店は中世の香り漂うブリュッセルの有名なグランプラスに面し、中世のファサードをもった建物内にある。外からでも店のオリジナリティーがはっきりと分かり、店の中に足を踏み入れると大胆なデザインで買物客を感動させるようなデザインが望まれた。

床から天井まで三角形の面で構成された壁面はチョコレート色で塗られ、買物客の気分を高揚させている。キュビズムの建築を想わせるこのスペースは、"チョコレートの石切場"をイメージし、石が刻まれるように作られた。壁面の上部と下部にはダイヤモンド面が付けられている。チョコレートの生地は途中で流れ、チョコレートの四角になり展示用のガラス棚に伸びている。店全体が未完のスペースとして捉えられ、インテリアは石切場の石が洗練された棚に変わっていくプロセスを表している。両側の二つの展示壁はチョコレート職人のショーケースで、職人の写真、経歴、彼らのメッセージ等が表示されている。

（上）店内左奥コーナーを見る

(Above) View of the corner at the left back

（右）デザインアプリケーション類

(Right) Design applications

（右右）イスもチョコレートのイメージ

(Right right) Stool also designed in the image of chocolate

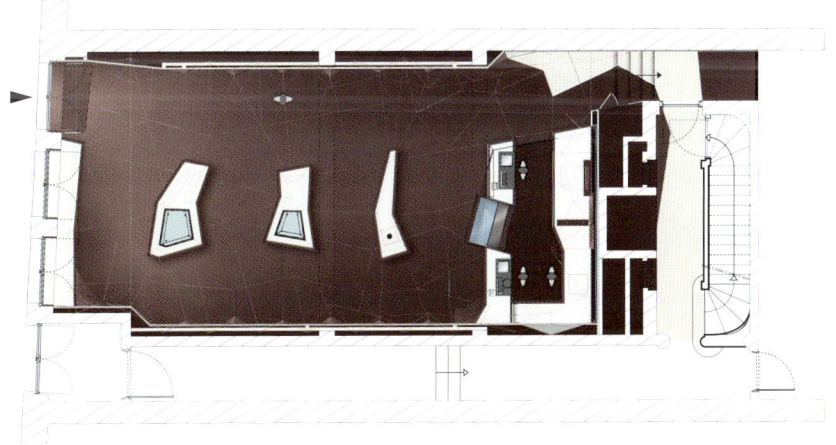

（上）店内奥のキャッシュ＆ラップエリア

(Above) Cash and wrap area at the inner of the store

Floor plan 1:150

The Best Belgian Chocolate of the World Association (BBCW) was interested in offering a platform to the country's Master Chocolatiers and creating a unique shop to promote fine Belgian chocolate. The concept was based on a design that appeals to the emotions, welcomes tastings, and allows for events to communicate the brand and to establish a showcase for people to find out more about the sweets. With a heavy scent of history, the shop faces Brussels' famous Grand Place and is situated in a building with a medieval façade. The originality of the boutique is evident even from the outside, and the concept required that the shop interior must strike the senses of the visitor with a bold design.

The floor-to-ceiling chocolate color treatment of the triangular retail space is designed to stir an emotional response. Evoking cubist architecture, the space suggests "a chocolate quarry," out of which the shop has been carved out.

Diamond-like facets are displayed on the upper and lower portions of the walls.

The chocolate materials give way in the middle to chocolate squares from which extend glass display shelves. Thus, the space reflects the transformation process, with crude rock from the quarry changing to the refinement of the displayed product. The store's two display walls offer a showcase to the resident chocolatiers, with his or her picture, curriculum vitae, birthplace, and personal quote.

Design firm: Minale Design Strategy
Designer: Gwenaël Hanquet, Jim Waters, Florence Balaes
Total area: 55 m²
Client: La Maison des Maîtres Chocolatiers Belges
Completion: Oct. 2009
Main materials: Linoléum®, Dark brown lacquered MDF, Dark brown painting
Site: Grand Place 4, 1000 Brussels

Elaborately Designed Food Shops - 2

Xocolatti

Chocolate store / New York

Designer: de-spec Inc.
Article: Ikunori Ara
Photography: Frank Oudeman

壁に残る客の痕跡

Design firm: de-spec Inc.
Designers: Farnaz Mansuri, Tom Shea
Consultant: Exit Creative
Client : Xocolatti
Total area: 13.5m²
Completion: Sep. 2011
Contractor: de-spec Inc.
Main materials: Bronze shelving system,
Walnut wood light boxes, Antique
driftwood flooring, Belgian bluestone
countertop, Metallic ceiling finish
Site : 72 Prince Street, New York

（左・上）ファサード

(Left, above) Facade

（上）ショーウィンドー越に見た店内全景
(Above) Full interior view through the show window

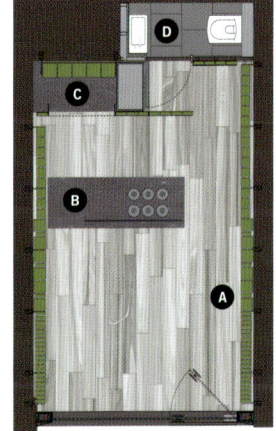

A: Chocolate Box shelves
B: Gelato counter
C: Back counter
D: WC

Floor plan 1:100

Xocolatti は高級チョコレートのニューブランドで、これはニューヨークのソーホーに出来た旗艦店である。ショップフロントやウインドーディスプレイ等の伝統的なバリアーを排除し、道路と境目のない一体感のある店舗を、わずか13.5m²の内に作ることがデザイナーの目論みであった。結果、店舗自体が高級チョコレートのショーケースのような店が通りに出現した。

壁は、床から天井までの特注ブロンズ製の棚システムによる整然とした線で構成されていて、数種類の異なるサイズの箱を収納できる。そのため、量的にも最大限のディスプレイと収納スペースの両方を兼ねた壁面となっている。顧客は気に入ったチョコレートボックスを取る結果、店内は一日

に幾通りもの壁パターンに変化する。客は、訪れるたびに異なった壁面グラフィックに出合うというわけである。このことはXocolattiとしても、どの商品がよく売れるか直ぐに分かり便利である。

デザイン協力の Exit Creative が、これらのチョコレートの商品説明のためにウォールナッツ材による棚のように飛び出した照明ボックスをデザインした。その棚の上の商品は、あたかも高価な宝石のようである。チョコレートを意識した茶色と緑色は、メタリックな天井まで店舗全体に溢れ、ブランドアイデンティティーを強く発信している。

Xocolatti is a new premium chocolate brand and this is its flagship store in Soho, New York. Within this 150ft² (13.5m²) store the designer's concept was to eliminate the traditional barriers of a storefront and window display, instead to create a shop that seamlessly integrates with the street. The result was a store that almost appears like a glass display case for the luxury chocolate.

The walls are lined with a custom designed floor to ceiling bronze shelving system that is based on the multiple variations of the different sizes of the chocolate boxes. The wall acting as both storage and display maximises the space available. Customers choose their favourite chocolate boxes and take them out of the wall resulting in multiple patterns that change throughout the day making the wall graphics unique every day. This is also useful for Xocolatti to see instantly the customer's preferred products. Designed in collaboration with Exit Creative within the box wall there are also projecting glowing walnut wood light boxes showcasing the handmade chocolates as if they are precious gems on display. These boxes inspire the customer to interact within the living wall grid. The whole shop is filled with hues of green and rich brown, from the floor to ceiling boxes to the metallic green ceiling finish, which perfectly communicates the brand's identity.

（上）壁面ディスプレイ・ディテール

(Above) Detail of the wall display

（下）壁面ディスプレイは幾通りものパターンに変化する

(Bottom) Graphics of the wall display changes into multiple patterns

フレームアップされた
特別なオリーブオイル

Elaborately Designed Food Shops - 3

TA-ZE

Premium olive oils store / Toronto

Designer: Burdifilek
Article: Yasuhiko Taguchi
Photography: Ben Rahn, A Frame Inc

（上）入口より店内を見る

(Above) View from the entrance

（右）店内右奥を見る

(Above) View of the inner right side in the store

Feature 2:　　　　　　　　　　　　　Elaborately Designed Food Shops

Design firm: Burdifilek
Designer: Paul Filek, Diego Burdi
Total area: 69.5 m²
Contractor: Century Group Inc.
Client: A'tolia Inc
Completion : Aug. 2011
Main materials: Matte black powder coated frames,
Floor to ceiling smoked glass cabinets,
Stone mosaic flooring,
Wood detailing, and solid marble countertops
Site: 120 Adelaide Street West, Toronto

トロントにオープンしたプレミアム・オリーブオイルのチェーン店。80㎡のこぢんまりしたサイズだが清潔な感じで専門店らしく整頓され、グルメ愛好家やレストランのシェフに支持されている。

TA-ZEはトルコ語でフレッシュを意味し、企業はオリーブオイルの製造で長い伝統を持っている。その製品はトルコ・エーゲ海地方の6地域、28,000人のオリーブ生産者を統括する33の共同製作者を通じて入ってくる。

インテリアは、このブランドの歴史と商品の健全性をイメージさせるような落ち着いたものが求められた。デザイナーは商品自体が持つ美しさに着目し、これとインテリア素材やフォルムが補い合い強調するようなデザインを心掛けた。

商品がよく見えるようにマットブラックに塗装した壁面の展示フレームは、オリーブオイル、オリーブ、ビネガーを効果的に浮いているように見せている。透明ガラスのキャビネットは収納スペースと目立つホリゾントの二役をこなしている。その奥のキャビネットにはプレミアム・オリーブオイルが保管されている。二つの大理石カウンターが一列に並べられ、一つはキャッシャーカウンターに、もう一つは販売員が商品の質や特色を説明する際のテイスティングバーになっている。

Opening in Toronto is TA-ZE, a chain of retail stores focusing on premium olive oils. Although just 80 square-meters in size, it is a clean and organized specialty shop popular with food enthusiasts and gourmet chefs alike.

With is name meaning "fresh" in Turkish, TA-ZE is rooted in the long traditions of olive-oil production. Its products hail from six provinces in the Aegean region of Turkey, from 33 co-operatives that count more than 28,000 olive producers. The calm interior reflects the history of the brand and the healthiness of the product. The designer focused on the beauty of the product itself and aimed for a design that emphasizes the form and materials that complements the product offering.

High-contrast, matte black frames float in the foreground, showcasing the olive oil, olive, and vinegar products. Clear glass cabinets function both as a storage space and a feature wall. The cabinets hold premium olive oil and are located at the back of the store. Two marble counters are located together, one serving as a cashier's desk, the other functioning as a tasting bar where a sales consultant can explain the quality and characteristics of the products.

（左上）店内最奥部ストック棚を見る

(Left Above) Stock shelves at the inner part in the store

（上）店内入り口右側を見る

(Above) View of the right side in the store from the entrance

（左下）店内左奥を見る

(Left Bottom) View of the inner left side in the store

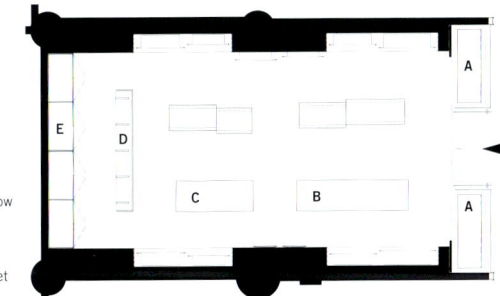

A: Show window
B: Tasting bar
C: Casher
D: Stock
E: RFR Cabinet

Floor plan 1:150

ワインを探索しながら奥へ進む
光りのカーヴ

Elaborately Designed Food Shops - 4

Mistral Wine Store

Wine & Champagne bar / Sao Paulo

Designer: Studio Arthur Casas
Article: Ikunori Ara
Photography: Fernando Guerra

（上）エントランスまわり外観

(Above) Exterior view around the entrance

（右）店内中央部の対面販売カウンター

(Right) Consultation counter at the center of the store

Feature 2:

Elaborately Designed Food Shops

（右）入口側より店内を見る

(Right) View from the entrance side

店内右奥のブックコーナー
Book corner at the right side back of
the store

Feature 2:   Elaborately Designed Food Shops

（上）中2階のテイスティング・バー

(Above) Tasting bar on the mezzanine

ワイン販売大手のMistralは、顧客をワインの世界へ引き込むような新しい企画の店舗をデザイナーに依頼した。Mistralの販売はほとんどがインターネットであるが、新規顧客やワイン愛好家を惹きつける遊び心あふれるワインやシャンペンのショーケースが欲しかった。

与えられたのは、天井は高いがわずか100m²のスペースである。そこに販売スペース、ワイン貯蔵室、倉庫、インタラクティブなギャラリー、関連本の読書室、テースティングのスペースが必要であった。そこで建築家は曲線の通路を作り、これらの要素が徐々に現れるようにレイアウトした。ボトルは浮遊しているかのように壁面の穴に差し込まれている。このオーガニックなラインの壁面は照明が内蔵され、上部はエレンガントで際だった雰囲気を持たせた縦格子で出来ている。全ての技術的設備的な機器はこの壁面内に納められている。この通路からガラスドアーで隔てた2層分の高さがあるワイン貯蔵室は、希少なワインを保管するため別の空調システムを設置している。通路の奥まったところには厳選されたワインを紹介する対面式のテーブルもある。店舗奥の縦格子は本棚になっていて、ワインテースティングは中2階で行なえる。

色彩計画は、木をメインに、白ツヤ有りのプラスチック壁面と黒ミラー張り壁面である。これらミニマルで、ソフィスティケートされた感覚による店で、ワインはアートギャラリーの展示品のようである。

Feature 2:   Elaborately Designed Food Shops

Design firm: Studio Arthur Casas
Designer: Arthur Casas
Co-authors: Raphael França, Joana Oliveira
Project manager: Cristiane Trolesi
Project team: Gabriel Ranieri, Maria Alice Carvalho, Mariana Santoro
Client: Mistral
Total area: 126.73 m²
Completion: Jun. 2012

Contractor: Souza Lima
Consultants: Studio Serradura- Lighting; Art des Caves- Cellar; K2P- Plumbing and Electrical engineering; SuperUber- Technology; Futurebrand- Visual Communication
Main materials: Wood(Oak) lath, Black mirror, High gloss white plastic, Steel structure
Site: Shopping JK, Sao Paulo

（上）店内最奥部ショーウィンドー近くの
対面販売カウンター

(Above) Consultation counter near the
show window at the back of the store

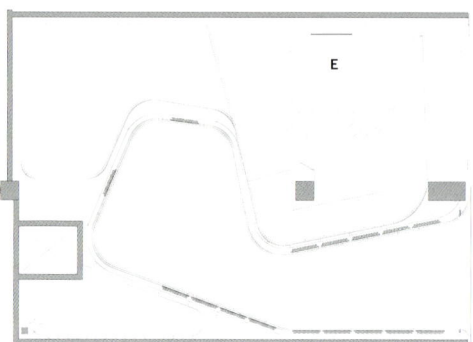

2nd floor plan

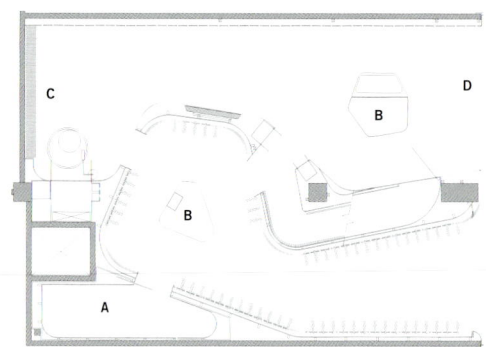

A: Wine cave
B: Consultaion counter
C: Book shelves
D: Show window
E: Tasting Bar

1st floor plan 1:200

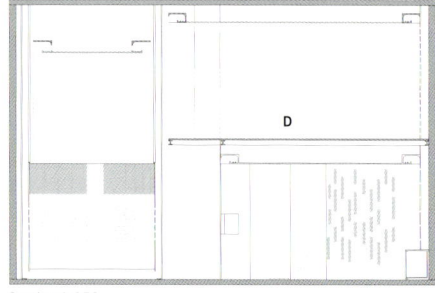

Section 1:150

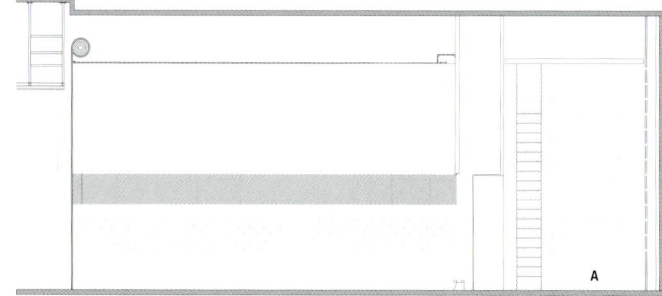

The wine distributor Mistral asked the designer to create a store in Sao Paulo, Brazil that would innovate the way clients approach the wine world. With most of their sales on the Internet they wanted to showcase wine and champagne in a recreational way attracting new customers and connoisseurs alike.

The space had a high ceiling and was only 100 m² but there needed to be sales space, cellar, storage, interactive gallery, reading room and wine tasting. Therefore the architects used a curve to create a path where the spaces appear gradually. Suspended bottles, held in the wall by cut out holes appearing to be floating, follow the organic shape,

formed by a backlight topped by a wood lath giving the store an elegant and discrete atmosphere. All the technical equipment is hidden within the walls. Separated from the main corridor by a glass door a double height cellar has its own air conditioning system to store rare wines. The store has an interactive table to showcase selected wines. The wood laths form a bookshelf at the back of the store and a tasting space was created in the mezzanine. The colour palette is simple with wood being the main material with high gloss white plastic and black mirror. With its minimalist, sophisticated stylish feel in this store wine is revered like works of art in a gallery.

Elaborately Designed Food Shops - 5

The Grapy Store

Wine shop / Roosendaal

Designer: Storeage
Article: Yasuhiko Taguchi
Photography: Dim Balsem

ワインのための
ユニット式ディスプレイボックス

きるような形にし、ワインを消費者にとって一層身
近なものにするコンセプトを作った。25㎡の店は
矢形にスタッキングして、組み変えることができる
展示ボックスのモジュールシステムで構成されてい
る。積み重なった色彩豊かなユニットは高さが異
なり、グレイビーのウェブサイト上にあってキャラ
クターづけられた、味を表にした"デジタルなソム
リエ"をまねている。
中央に置かれたユニットは消費者が料理のタイプ
をタッチスクリーンに打ち込むことで、店で購入で
きる最適なワインを見つけられるものである。ソム
リエによって選ばれたワインは積み重ね展示シス
テムの一番上のユニットにあり、下のエリアはワイ
ンの保管ユニットとして使われている。チョークボー
ドペイントで価格やPOPを直接ユニットに描ける
ようにデザインされた。

ワインのオンライン販売会社グレイビーがオランダ、
ローゼンダールのパッサージュ・モールに出店した。
店は、食べ物とワインを結びつけることで相乗効
果を得るため、同じ店舗区画内にある本屋の料
理本コーナーに隣接して出店された。
デザイナーは融通性のある展示方法で、周囲の店、
本屋、グルメデリ、CDショップなどと共存共栄で

（上）本屋側入口より見る

(Above) View from the book shop side
entry

Feature 2:

Elaborately Designed Food Shops

（左）壁側の展示ユニット

(Left) Wall-side mounting type display units

（上）スタッキングできるアイランドタイプ
展示ユニット

(Above) Stackable island type display units

Online wine retailer Grapy.nl opened its first physical store at the Passage Mall in Roosendaal, The Netherlands.
Taking advantage of the inseparable pairing of food and wine, the Grapy Store is located in the same space as a bookstore, next to its cooking section. The designer selected an integrated display approach, allowing co-existence with the bookstore, gourmet deli, and CD shop, and created a concept that brings wine closer to consumers.
The 25 square-meter store features a modular system of arrow-shaped and stackable, changeable wine and book units. The stacks of colorful units differ in height, recalling the digital sommelier flavor charts on the Grapy website.
An interactive touch screen on the centrally-placed unit allows customers to type in their food choices and find complimentary wines in the store. The top unit of the stackable system contains an adaptable display area that allows wine bottles to be shown as if presented by a sommelier, and the lower units are used to store large amounts of wine. Chalkboard paint permits pricing and other details to be written directly on the units.

Feature 2:   Elaborately Designed Food Shops

（左上）アイランドタイプ展示ユニットを
通じて壁面展示を見る

(Left above) Wall-side displays viewed
over the island display units

（右上）パサージュ・モール側の外観

(Right above) Exterior view from the
Passage Mall

Basic Unit

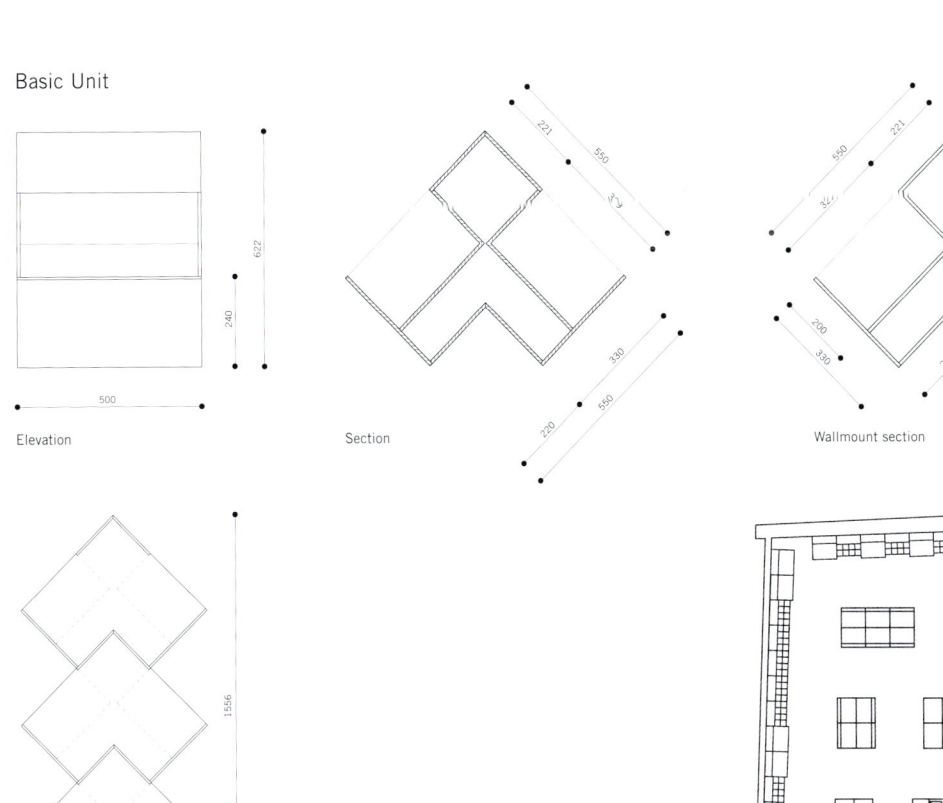

Elevation

500

622

240

Section

221   550

330

550   220

Wallmount section

550   221

467

200

330   220

Keeplat

Stacking

1556

778

Design firm: Storeage
Designer: Leendert Tange- Partner and
co-founder
Joao Carneiro- Designer
Sarah Napier- Graphic designer
Total area: 25 m²
Client: Grapy.nl
Completion: Aug. 2011
Main materials: Wood
Site: Passage Mall in Roosendaal, The
Netherlands

A: Entry through shoping mall
B: Entry through book shop

Floor plan 1:150

Elaborately Designed Food Shops - 6

VyTA Boulangerie Italiana

Boulangerie / Torino

パンから導かれたインテリアイメージ

Designer: Daniela Colli
Article: Masaatsu Fukazawa
Photography: Matteo Piazza

（上）左側エントランスまわり外観

(Above) View around the left side entrance

（左）イートインエリアを通してエントランス方向見返し

(Left) Looking back at the entrance through the eat in area

右側エントランスよりパン売場を見る

View of the bread showcase from the
right side entrance

（上）バール
(Above) Bar

Feature 2:

パン屋は古代エジプトや古代ローマからある古い業種であるが、近年イタリアなどではスーパーなどに押されて減る傾向にある。

この店はイタリアにおいて新しくチェーン展開しているパン屋で、業態開発によって時代にマッチしたパン屋を目指している。営業戦略的に主要駅構内に展開していて、この店はトリノのポルタ・ヌオヴァ駅構内にある。各種のパンをベースに軽食を提供し、メニューはパニーノ、サンドイッチ、ピザ、菓子パン、デザートなど、そして飲み物である。

インテリアは黒をベースにしたクールな空間で、素材的に人工材と自然材の統合を試みたとデザイナーは言う。黒い床や壁、カウンター、天井、これにオーク材による二つのデザイン要素を対比させている。一つはオーク板で出来た緩いカーブを描く板の交互の並置で、パンを盛る藤などで編んだ伝統的バスケットからヒントを得たものである。網目を建築的スケールまで拡大し象徴化し天井から垂れたフードとしている。二つ目はイタリアの伝統的なパンの一つ、ロゼッタの表面の切れ込みからヒントを得、オーク材で黒地の上に多角的断片の形を壁にあしらっている。

カウンターは黒のコーリアンとガラスのショーケースの組み合わせで、商品をそのまま見せ、飲み物もその上でサービスする。近年イタリアで普及してきたサービススタイルである。

また不定形にデザインされたミツバチの巣のような六角形のテーブルは、グループ客などへ組み合わせがフレキシブルである。

照明に浮かび上がるこの場は劇場舞台のようで、客は出演者であり観客でもあるような場を作りだしている。

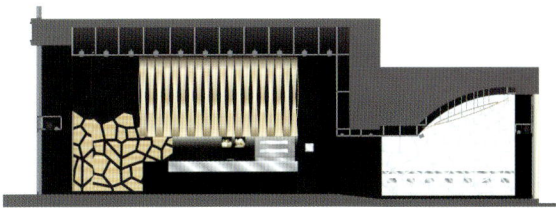

Section

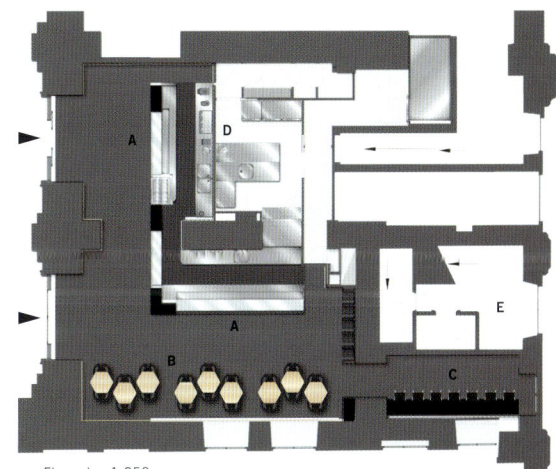

A: Bread SC
B: Eat in
C: Bar
D: Kitchen
E: Stair well

Floor plan 1:250

（上）右側エントランスよりバール方向を見る

(Above) View towards the bar from the right side entrance

Design firm: Colli Daniela Architetto s.r.l.
Design team: Daniela Colli, Francesco Belvedere
Constructor: arcHITect s.r.l.
Total area: 150 m²
Clien: Retail food s.r.l.
Completion: Aug. 2011
Construction phase: Apr.–Aug. 2011
Main materials: Floor- High quality fine porcelain stoneware size 60x120cm Polished black,
Ceiling- black painted plasterboard
Site: Torino Porta Nuova railway station, via Sacchi, Torino

Bakeries are one of the oldest businesses that have existed since the times of ancient Egypt and Rome. But in recent Italy, bakeries have decreased in number as supermarkets selling mass-produced bread have been taking over their place.

This bakery is developing its chain store network in Italy in a style that meets the trend of the time. As its business strategy, it opens stores within the major railway station buildings. This store is inside the Porta Nuova railway station building in Torino. In addition to a variety of bread, it serves light meals such as paninos, sandwiches, pizzas, pastries, desserts and drinks.

Its interior is a cool space with black as the base, and intended to be an integration of man-made and natural materials, according to the designer. Two elements made of oak are used in contrast to the black floor, walls, counter, table, and ceiling. One is the juxtaposition of softly curved oak planks which evoke the image of a traditional interwoven bread basket. The mesh size has been expanded into an architectural scale to symbolically use the planks as a hood hanging from the ceiling. The second one is the use of irregularly cut oak planks as a wall material. It comes from "rosette," a typical kind of bread in Italy the surface of which looks like rose petals.

The counter is the combination of black Corian and glass showcase. Products are shown in the case, and drinks are served on the case. This style of service is becoming popular in Italy.

The hexagonal tables can be flexibly combined for groups with a large number of people.

When lit, the space becomes like a theatrical stage on which customers become actors as well as audience.

ソリッドなヨーグルトのカウンター

（上）イートイン席より見る

(Above) View from the eat-in area

（左）外観

(Left) Exterior view

Elaborately Designed Food Shops

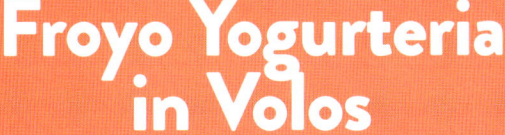

Froyo Yogurteria in Volos

Frozen Yogurt Bar / Volos, Greece

Designer: **Ahylo Studio**
Article: **Ikunori Ara**
Photography: **Ioulietta Zindrou** (Ahylo Studio)

（右）ヨーグルトカウンターをサイドより
見る

(Right) Side view of the Yogurt counter

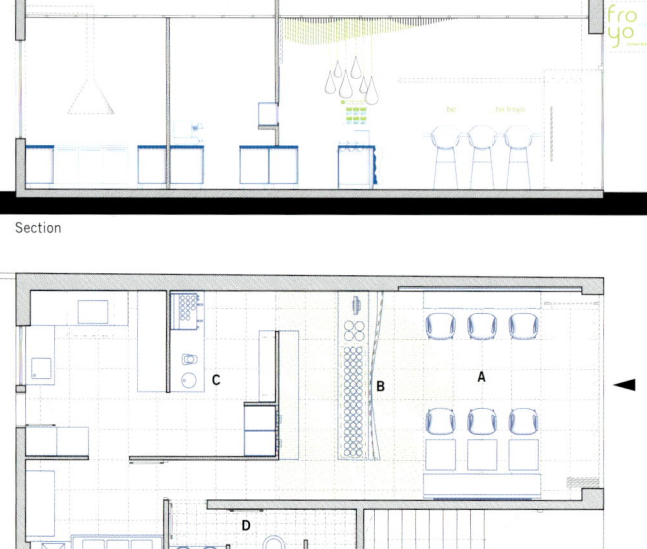

（上）ヨーグルトカウンター俯瞰   （下）入り口より見る

(Above) Overlooking the Yogurt counter   (Bottom) View from the entrance

A: Eat-in
B: Gelato counter
C: Kitchen
D: WC

Section

Floor plan 1:150

Feature 2:

Ahylo Studioが、ギリシャの冷凍ヨーグルト・チェーンFroyo Yogurteriaのためにフランチャイズショップをデザインした。求められたのは、ここの商品の特徴であるヨーグルトの品質、新鮮度、色彩、テクスチャーを反映した材料や色をピックアップしてデザインにすることであった。ヨーグルトのトッピングのカウンターと天井デザインにそれがよく現れている。

カウンターの前面は波打った曲線の仕上げで、これがヨーグルトの壁とすれば、ケースの中のトッピングたちは顧客の前でじらすように魅力的に展示されている、というわけだ。

二次曲線の強調された天井は、ヨーグルトの起源である牧草を連想させるよう、新鮮なグリーンに塗装されている。また、コンパクトFLを使用した真っ白の照明器具は、天井からしたたるミルクの滴のようである。中間色のセラミックフロアタイル、白と緑の椅子、木のベンチシート、カウンター上の木貼り、白色の壁面は、シンプルさと清潔感を出すために選ばれ、主役のヨーグルト・カウンターを際立たせている。

Elaborately Designed Food Shops

Ahylo Studio has designed a franchise shop for the Greek frozen yogurt chain Froyo Yogurteria in Volos, Greece. The brief was for the design to highlight the product's qualities, thus the freshness, the colour and the texture of yogurt are reflected in the choice of materials and colours. The yogurt toppings counter and the ceiling are the main elements used to show this. The front side of the counter is finished with wavy carved lines as if 'a wall of yogurt' with the toppings displayed tantalizingly in front of the customer. The spatial identity of the store is emphasized with a double curvature ceiling painted with the fresh green colour of the brand, referencing the natural origins of yogurt. Lights with pure white compact florescent bulbs appear as 'milk drops' dropping from the ceiling. The neutral ceramic floor tiles, small seating area with a wooden banquet and seats of white and green, wood above the counter and plain white walls were again chosen for their simplicity and clean feel and do not detract from the main elements.

Design firm: Ahylo Studio
Designer: Pavlos Xanthopoulos, Ioulietta Zindrou
Graphic design: Asprimera Design Studio
Client: Froyo yogurteria Volos
Total area: 70 m²
Completion: Aug. 2012
Contractor: Froyo yogurteria / branding
Main materials: Floor- Light grey ceramic tile,
Wall- White paint finish, Ceiling- Lacquered wood,
Counter- Lacquered wood
Site: 8 Glavani str, Volos, Greece

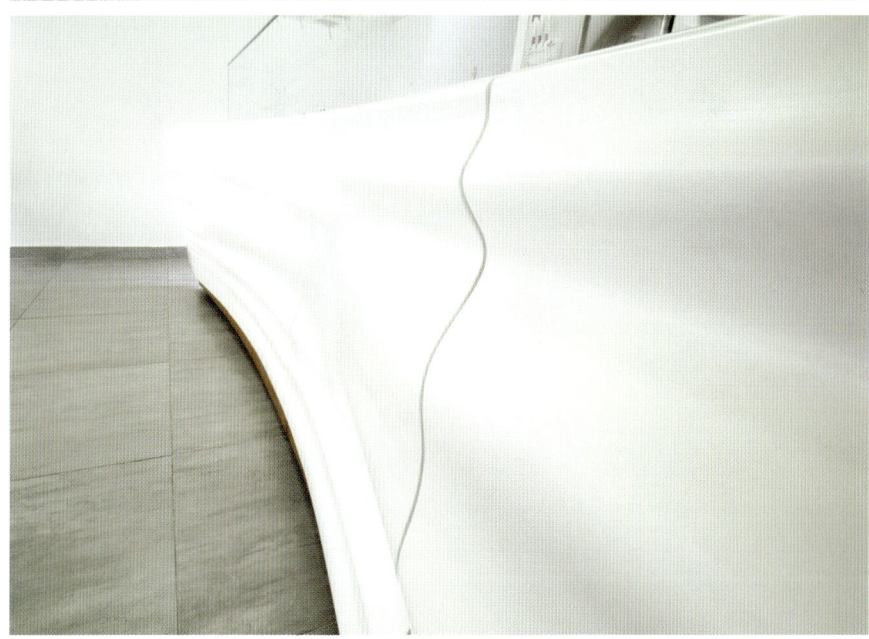

（上）ヨーグルトカウンターの天井ディテール

(Above) Detail of the ceiling at the Yogurt counter

（下）ヨーグルトカウンター・ディテール

(Bottom) Detail of the Yogurt counter

Elaborately Designed Food Shops - 8

Ice Cream Castle

Ice cream shop / Akershus, Norway

Designer: Scenario Interior Architects
Article: Ikunori Ara
Photography: Gatis Rozenfelds / F64

氷原にほどばしる
アイスクリームのメルヘン

エントランスより見た全景
Whole interior view from the entrance

Feature 2:

Elaborately Designed Food Shops

Gelato counter

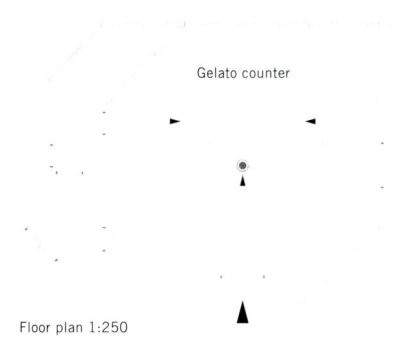

Floor plan 1:250

（左上）氷原をイメージした床

(Left above) Floor in the image of an ice-field

（右上）アイスクリーム・カウンターより見る

(Right above) View from the ice cream counter

Design firm: Scenario Interior Architects
Project responsible: Linda Steen
Project leader: Tine Haaland-Paulsen
Co-design team: Nichlas Hoel, Are Fredrik Berg
Client: Diplom-is
Total area: 100 ㎡
Completion: Apr. 2012
Main materials: Ceiling- MDF cut by CNC technology
Site: Tusenfryd – a amusement park in Akershus, Norway

Diplom-isはノルウェーのアイスクリーム会社。Akershusの遊園地内にある彼らの直営店舗は，新しいイメージによる改装を必要としていた。デザイナーは短期間の上、少ない予算で、楽しめるワンダーランドを子供達のためにつくらなければならなかった。

立てられたデザインコンセプトは「Diplom-isのマスコットのエスキモーが、色のない北極圏に飽き、氷に穴を開け幾つかの色を北極圏に追加した。それらは、まるで爆発したように辺り一面に飛び散った」というもので、このストーリーがインテリアやグラフィックに反映された。

店内中央の柱をストローに見立て、ストロベリー、チョコレート、ピスタチオ、マンゴより選んだ色を使用し、その解けたアイスクリームが噴水のように天井へ飛び散ったというイメージである。既存の壁が活かされ、ストーリーのグラフィックを施し、また子供が届き易いよう小さなスロープを取付けたカウンターは、氷の面をイメージした床に浮かばせた。加えてペンギンのキャラクターも氷の上で踊らせている。店舗の外装はバニラアイス色に塗られ、周囲の遊園地環境とコントラストを保ち、店の内外共に「氷の城」となっている。

Diplom-is, a Norwegian ice cream company, wanted to re-brand and refurbish their ice cream shop in an amusement park in Akershus, Norway. With very little time to complete and a very tight budget the designer was commissioned to create a fun wonderland for children. The concept for the shop was inspired by a story about ' Eskimonia 'a Diplom-is mascot. She was bored of living in the colourless North Pole so drilled a hole in the ice to add some colour. Like an explosion all the flavours burst out of the hole and coloured all the surrounding area. The interior and graphics reflect this story. The column in the middle is a straw sucking up all the flavours of strawberry, chocolate, pistachio and mango thus the colour palette was chosen. This 'melted ice cream' then splashes onto the ceiling like a fountain. The existing walls were kept and covered with the story graphics. On the floor 'sheets of ice' were laid and a small wooden platform was made in front of the counter so the children could reach. As a further element of fun penguins were added to dance on the ice. The entire building surface is vanilla coloured, which serves as a contrast to the surrounding park landscape and becomes an ice castle inside and out.

（上）ファサード
(Above) Facade

Elaborately Designed Food Shops - 9

Coffee Bar, Montgomery

Café / San Francisco, USA

高機能でサービスされる
高品質のコーヒー

（下）アーケードに面したコーヒーバー

(Bottom) Coffee bar facing the arcade

Designer: jones | haydu
Article: Ikunori Ara
Photography: Bruce Damonte

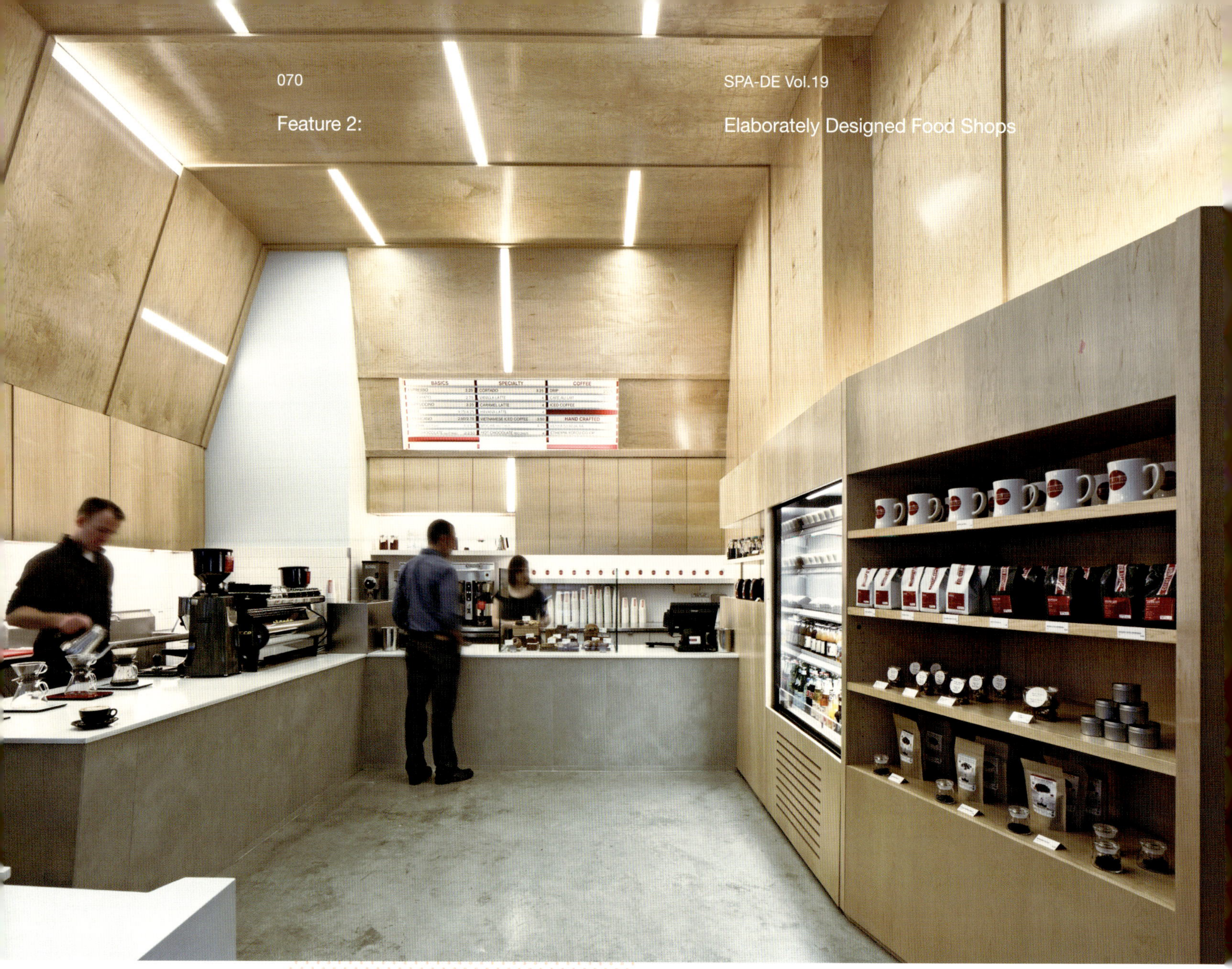

（上）入口より店内を見る

（下）店内左奥を見る

(Above) View from the entrance

(Bottom) View of the left side in the store

A: Arcade
B: RFR. Case
C: Counter
D: Kitchen

Floor plan

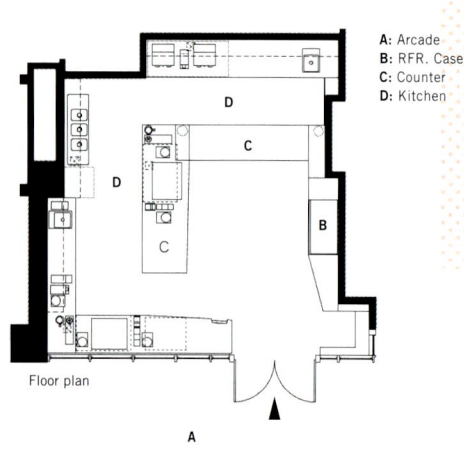

Feature 2:

Coffee Bar Montgomeryはサンフランシスコのビジネス街に位置している。以前は倉庫だったわずか45m²ほどの広さで、建築的な特色もなく、高天井で床から天井までのガラスファサードを持つスペースに店は作られた。ショップとしては、高品質の良いコーヒーを早く提供することがこのエリアでのビジネスとして要求された。そのため、客席よりもバリスタ（コーヒー淹れ職人）が快適に仕事できる効果的な広さをカウンター内に作ることが優先された。その上、そのスペースを外からオープンにして、まるでコーヒーを作ることが劇場の一場面のようにエスプレッソマシーンを中央ステージに配置した。

マテリアルの数を極力少なくし、狭いスペースがごみごみしないように注意を払い、壁と天井は表面仕上げ済みの1200mm x 2400mmのメープル合板を選び、温かさとコストダウンを計った。この合板仕上げは人造石 White Caesarstone のカウンターの高さまでアーチ状に下がって来て、4mの豊かな天井高を強調している。カウンターの前面にはセラミックタイルが貼られ、床のコンクリートの色とマッチさせた。そして省エネタイプの照明器具が、互い違いに壁から天井にかけて水平に取付けられ、まるでかがり火のように、歩道から店内へ顧客を呼び込んでいる。

The Coffee Bar Montgomery is situated in the financial district of downtown San Francisco. Originally for storage the space was small under 500sqf with no real distinctive architectural features just a tall ceiling and full height glass storefront. The brief was the shop had to provide premium coffee at a speed that could meet the fast pace of this area. Therefore it was decided it was more important to have more baristas with space to work comfortably and efficiently behind the counter rather than seating. Also keeping the space open the coffee making is like a theatrical experience with the espresso machine as centre stage.

The number of materials was kept to a minimum so as not to overwhelm the small space. For the walls and ceiling standard 4' x 8' sheets of prefinished maple plywood were chosen for its warmth and low cost. This wood drapes down in a dramatic arch to meet the white caesarstone counter, highlighting the 14' plus ceiling height of the space. The counter front is clad in porcelain tiles to match the colour of the concrete floor. The high efficiency light fixtures, horizontally interspersed through the wall and ceiling create a glowing wood shell that serves as a beacon to draw in and welcome pedestrians to the store.

Design Firm: jones | haydu
Designer: Hulett Jones and Paul Haydu
Area: 約45 m²
Open: Jan. 2012
Contractor: Northern Sun
Client: Coffee Bar
Main Materials: Floor- Concrete floor, Wall & Ceiling- Maple plywood, Cabinetry- Maple plywood, Countertop- White Caesarstone, Counter Front- Porcelain tile
Site: 101 Montgomery Street, San Francisco

（左上）天井を見上げる

(Left above) Looking up at the ceiling

（右上）店内右側を見る

(Right above) View of the right side in the store

Designer: 3six0 Architecture
Article: Yasuhiko Taguchi
Photography: 3six0 Architecture

Bel Frites

フライドポテト・キオスクの
プロトタイプデザイン

（上・右）ショッピングモール内のBel
Frites キオスク

(Above, right) Bel Frites Kiosk in the
shopping mall

Feature 2:

Elaborately Designed Food Shops

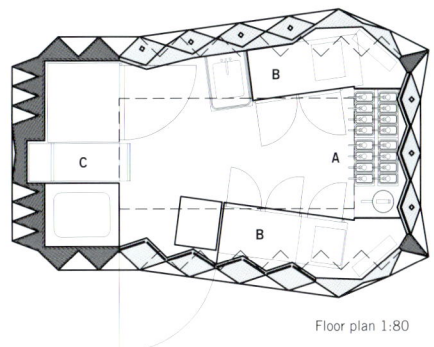

Floor plan 1:80

A: Sause & Topping dispenser
B: Beverage under counter
C: Electric Frier

Design firm: 3six0 Architecture
Designer: Christopher Bardt, Kyna Leski, Jack Ryan,
Total area: 12 m²
Contractor: Mystic Scenic Studios, Inc
Client: Riz Jamal
Completion: Oct. 2004
Main materials: Sheet copper wall surface, stainless steel plate counter-tops, clear and colored acrylic
Site: Multiple shopping mall locations – (Location shown: Square One Mall, Saugas, Massachusetts)

本場ベルギーのフレンチフライを提供するキオスクがショッピングモールのためにデザインされた。キオスクは独立したストラクチャーで、通気孔、調理台、冷蔵庫がビルトインされ、2人の従業員が働けるスペースから構成されている。キオスクは、モール内のどこに配置されるかによって1面、3面（壁面をバックに配置）、4面（フリースタンディング）のバリエーションをもっている。三つの異なったセッティングにおいて認知度を高め、一貫性のあるブランドイメージをつくることが重要であった。デザイナーはプリーツ状に折り曲げた幾何形体を使って、いろいろな状況に対応できるシンプルな建築的方法を開発した。サインはBel Fritesの文字を折り面に切り込んでストラクチャー本体に組み込んだ。買い物客が斜め方向から来てもベル・フリットの名前がはっきり読めるようになっている。本体は赤茶で存在感が出され、サインのオレンジと黄色でアクセントが付けられた。

A specialized kiosk for serving authentic Belgian fries was developed expressly for shopping mall environments. This kiosk can stand alone and features self-contained venting, cooking, and refrigeration equipment. Its working space is large enough for two employees.
The kiosk design depends on the location within the mall, with variations ranging from single face (in-line), three faces (against a wall) and four faces (freestanding). It was important for the brand that there was a recognizable and consistent image across all three settings.
Using folded, pleated geometry, the designer developed a simple architectural strategy that can adapt to various situations. Signage was integrated into the architecture by cutting the letters of the name "Bel Frites" into the folds. Even when customers approach at an angle, the name can be read clearly. The unit itself announces its presence with a red color with the orange and yellow of the sign adding accent.

（左上）キオスクを俯瞰する

(Left above) Overlooking the Kiosk

（右上）ディシャップカウンター

(Right above) Dish up counter

ハイスタイル・カジュアルな
ステーション・フードマーケット

Elaborately Designed Food Shops - 11

EKI MARCHÉ OSAKA Marche's Kitchen and Entrée Marché Osaka

Gourmet market / Osaka

Designer: Nomura Co.,Ltd
Photography: Yasunori Shimomura

（上）JR大阪駅エキマルシェ大阪口
(Above) JR Line Eki Marche Osaka Gate

（右）JR大阪駅桜橋口のコーナー外観
(Right) The corner exterior view around
JR Line Sakurabashi gate

（上）ファッションのエリア「ALBI」に接した Marche's Kitchen

(Above) Marché's Kitchen facing the fashon area ALBI

Marche's Kitchen

（左）飲食ゾーンMarche's Cafe & Dining 側からJR線エキマルシェ大阪口への通路を見通す

(Left) Passage way for the JR Line Eki Marche Osaka Gate viewed from Marche's Cafe & Dining side

（右上）洋菓子売り場

(Right above) Confectionary department

Feature 2:   Elaborately Designed Food Shops

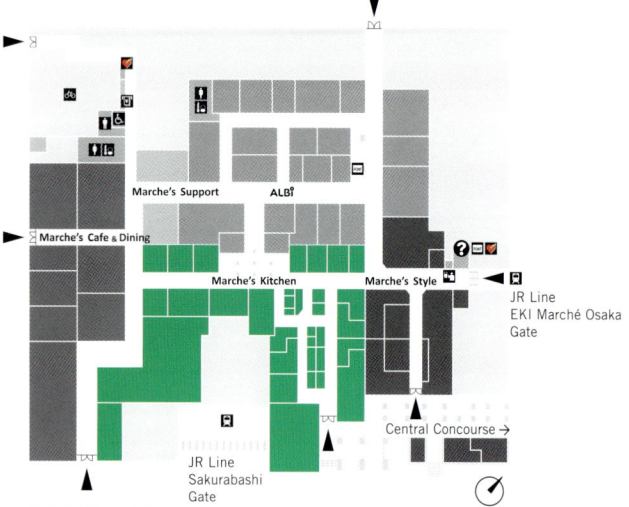

EKI Marché site map

A: Super Market (Deli Festa)
B: Boulangerie
C: Pretzel
D: Convenience store

（左上・右上）スーパーマーケット「Deli Festa」

(Left above, right above) Super market Deli Festa

（右下）飲食店ゾーンとの境の通路

(Right bottom) Passage way between Marche's Cafe & Dining and Marche's Kitchen

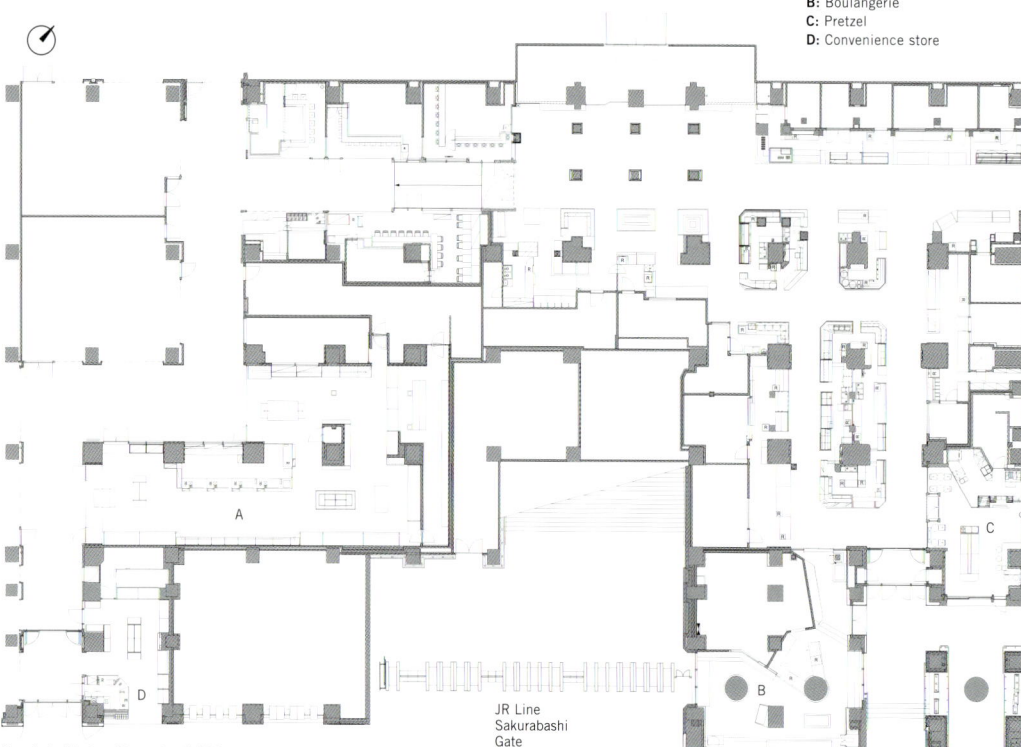

Marche's Kitchen Floor plan 1:500

〈エキマルシェ大阪 マルシェズ・キッチン 概要〉
デザイン：乃村工藝社
デザイナー：三瓶邦夫、岡崎理、吉谷武敏、出口智彦、川西英毅、築地原勲、村上みか、田中竜二
ディレクター：壺坂廣志
延べ床面積：7,200㎡（エキマルシェ大阪全体）
施工：大林組、大鉄工業、竹中工務店、錢高組、淺沼組、奥村組 特定建設工事共同企業体 + 乃村工藝社
クライアント：株式会社ジェイアール西日本デイリーサービスネット 他
竣工：2012年10月31日
工期：2012年1月〜9月
主な仕上げ材：大谷石チェーン挽き、不燃木（ヴィンテージウッド・米ツガうづくり）、杉柾網代籠目編み、カラーステンレス、磁器タイル
所在地：大阪市北区梅田3-1-1 JR大阪駅1F構内

[EKI MARCHÉ OSAKA Marche's Kitchen Data]
Design firm: Nomura Co.,Ltd
Designer: Mikame Kunio, Okazaki Osamu, Yoshitani Taketoshi, Deguchi Tomohiko, Kawanishi Hideki, Tsuichihara Isao, Murakami Mika, Tanaka Ryuuji
Director: Tsubosaka Hiroshi
Total area: 7,200 m²
Contractor: Obayashi,Daitetsu Kogyo,Takenaka,Zenitaka,Asanuma,Okumura JV+ Nomura Co.,Ltd
Client: West Japan Railway Daily Service Net Company Co.,Ltd
Project completion: Oct. 2012
Construction phase: Jan.–Sep. 2012
Site: 1F JR Osaka Station, 3-1-1, Umeda, Kita-ku, Osaka

Feature 2:   Elaborately Designed Food Shops

（右）キャッシャー前の食品売り場を見る

(Above) Food department in front of
the cashier

Entrée Marché Osaka

〈アントレマルシェ大阪 概要〉
設計施工：乃村工藝社
アートディレクター：山崎康正
デザイナー：吉谷武敏
ディレクター：壺坂廣志
床面積：423 ㎡
クライアント：株式会社ジェイアール西
日本デイリーサービスネット
竣工：2012年8月25日
工期：2012年1月～8月
主な仕上げ材：モザイクタイル、セラミッ
クタイル、木製モールディング、SUS.HL
所在地：大阪市北区梅田3-1-1 JR大
阪駅1F構内

[Entrée Marché Osaka Data]
Design firm and Contractor: Nomura
Co.,Ltd
Art director: Yamasaki Yasumasa
Designer: Yoshitani Taketoshi
Director: Tsubosaka Hiroshi
Total area: 423 m²
Client: West Japan Railway Daily Service
Net Company Co.,Ltd
Project completion: Aug. 2012
Construction phase: Jan.–Aug. 2012
Site: 1F JR Osaka Station, 3-1-1,
Umeda, Kita-ku, Osaka

A: Souvenir
B: Convenience sotre
C: Consignment store
D: Cashier
E: Refrigerator
F: Staff room

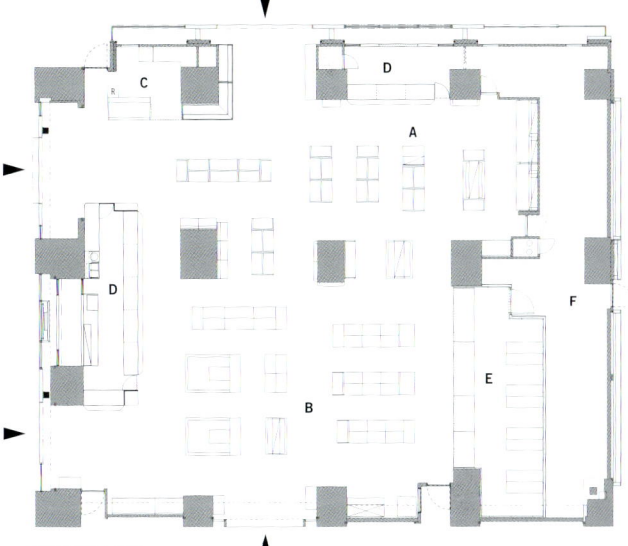

Floor plan 1:300

（上）中央コンコースに面した外観

(Above) Exterior view facing Central
concourse

Feature 2:

Elaborately Designed Food Shops

梅田の中心である大阪駅の西側に開業した「エキマルシェ大阪」はJR西日本エリア最大規模のエキナカ商業施設である。いわゆる「エキナカ」は、東京を始めとした関東圏では一つのビジネスモデルとして定着しつつあるが、関西やJR西日本エリアにおいては、まだまだこれからの状況である中、「エキマルシェ大阪」は今後のJR西日本グループの「エキナカ」ビジネスの新たなチャレンジの起点となる重要プロジェクトと位置付けられた。
場所は大阪ステーションシティの一角、桜橋口に隣接、JR線エキマルシェ大阪口に直結する駅構内で、食物販・グルメの「マルシェズ・キッチン」、飲食の「マルシェズ・カフェ&ダイニング」、コスメ・雑貨の「マルシェズ・スタイル」、ファッションの「ALBI」、サービスの「マルシェズ・サポート」の五つにゾーニングされている。ここに紹介する「マルシェズ・キッチン」は「エキマルシェ大阪」の中核的なゾーンである。

エキマルシェ大阪の施設コンセプトは「大人のみちくさ」。時間を有効に使いたいと考える大阪駅の全ての利用者に、"駅だからこそ"の「安心感」「利便性」に加え、"駅なのに"「楽しさ」「快適さ」「ちょっと幸せ」を感じてもらえる「"駅ならでは"の新たなデイリーニーズ」の創造を目指した。エキマルシェ大阪にさっと、ふらっと、ワクワクっと訪れてもらうこと、それが「大人のみちくさ」であり、このコンセプトを基に空間デザイン、MD等が計画された。全体の環境デザインコンセプトは「Cool Osaka」である。
「Cool Osaka」とは、はんなりとしたモダンな空間である。「はんなり」という言葉は「花なり」の略で、上品で、明るく華やかな様を表す。艶（つや）の大阪らしい飾り過ぎない生成り感覚を持たせるようにした。具体的には、要所に伝統や文化が薫る和テイストの杉柾網代籠目編み、割竹、日本固有の大谷石を配し、だれもが和める自然素材を効果的に織り込んだ明るく落ち着きのある空間を構成した。
また、同じ駅構内には、このプロジェクトとほぼ同時並行して進められた「アントレマルシェ大阪」があり、こちらはお土産とコンビニを一体化した大型店である。大阪駅利用客に求められるニーズに対応したワンストップショッピング型の店舗で、デザインも「Bright Crystal Stage」をコンセプトに、明快なVMDと共に、大阪らしい"派手さ"と"際立つ存在感"をアピールした。
いずれもJR西日本グループの「エキナカ」ビジネスのこれからを見据え、今までにないものを求める姿勢で取り組んだ。〈三瓶邦夫＋吉谷武敏〉

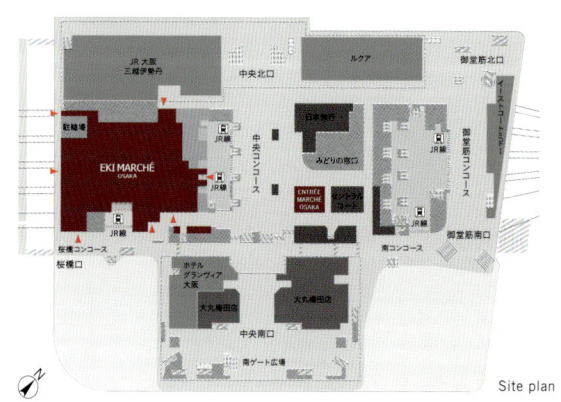

Site plan

（上）店内中央部付近
(Above) Central part of the store

Eki Marché Osaka in the western part of Osaka railway station is the largest commercial complex in the area covered by West Japan Railway Company (JR West). Operating shops and restaurants inside railway stations is already a common business model in the Greater Tokyo area. However, it is not well established in Kansai and western Japan. JR West considers the Eki Marché Osaka as an important start of its new business development.
It is located in a corner of the Osaka Station City, and is directly connected to the Eki Marché Osaka exit of the JR lines. The Eki Marché Osaka is largely divided into five zones. The Marché's Kitchen is in the central zone of the Marché. The concept of the Eki Marché Osaka was to provide adults with places for loitering on their way to and from their destinations. We intended to create a place to meet the daily needs of all users of Osaka Station who want to make efficient use of their time by providing them with a safe and convenient shopping area, and moreover, pleasure, comfort and a little bit of happiness by being in the area. We planned its spatial design and merchandising under this concept. The concept for environmental design is "Cool Osaka." It suggests an elegant, bright and colorful modern space. Our intention was to create it to be sophisticated, not being too decorative but simple with the touch of unbleached and undyed cloth. We installed wickerwork objects made of Japanese cedar tree, cut bamboo trees, and Oya stone here and three to give Japanese traditional flavors. With these natural materials, the interior was created to make people feel relaxed.
Within the same station, there is Entrée Marché Osaka. It is a large one-stop store combining a souvenir shop and a convenience store to meet the needs of users of the station. The design concept for this store was "a bright crystal stage." Together with a clear visual merchandising, a "flashy and outstanding" design was sought to reflect Osaka people's mood.
We approached them seeking novelty as a launching project of successive business inside station houses by JR West.

SPA-DE Vol.19

World
Spatial
Design

世界の空間デザイン

Masrah Al Qasba
Theatre

Theater / Sharjah, United Arab Emirates

Designer:
magma architecture

Article: Yasuhiko Taguchi
Photography:Torsten Seidel

客席から舞台を見る
Stage viewed from the 3rd floor seating

砂丘の風紋

2階レベル舞台袖エントランスより見る
View of the seating from the entrance
to the wing of the stage

アルカサバ劇場の改装にあたってデザインに求められたのは、モダンな劇場にすることと、過去の日常生活をさりげない雰囲気の中にうまく融け込ませることであった。クライアントはまた、将来への文化的要素を取り入れ、シャラジャ首長国の自然と歴史に根付いた劇場を求めた。

遊牧の時代において、ニュースは広い砂漠の中で声を出して伝えられた。この劇場のデザインはそんなシャラジャの自然を表し、遠近感のある風景を暗示している。波型の面は折られた線に沿って照明が付けられ、まるで夕日が砂山に色を投影したようなイメージで天井に散りばめられた。劇場にやって来る人々は日常の生活から離れ、劇場の空間に語られている思いがけない印象的なスペースに浸ることができる。

過去と現在は材料の選択においても反映され、インテリアの表面はハイテックで現代的な印象であるにもかかわらず、この地方の伝統的な建築材料であるテキスタイルから作られている。テキスタイルは300席の劇場の壁、天井を連続したなめらかな面で包んでいる。

折り面のラインにある照明は二重になっている曲面に上品なアクセントを与え、照明は観客の目がまぶしくないように席からは見えないようにデザインされている。面の割れ目に取り付けられたスポットライトは講演やトークショー時等のために明るさを調整することができる。

ロビーと控室は劇場スペースと対比させ、白と柔らかい照明で訪問者が寛げる空間にデザインされた。

（上）「砂丘の照明」と名付けられた天井のスリットライト

(Above) Slit light at the ceiling called Dune Lights

（下）客席最上部より舞台を見る

(Bottom) Overlooking the stage from the uppermost seating

（左上）天井のノングレア・ライティング
のディテール

(Above) Detail of the non glaring ceiling light

（右上）劇場の外観

(Right above) Whole exterior view of
the theatre

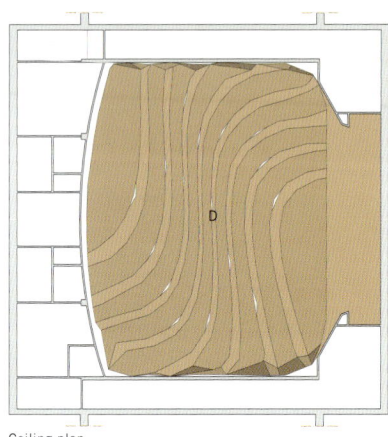

A: Foyer
B: VIP area
C: Auditorium entrance
D: Auditorium
E: Stage
F: Green room
G: Storage room foyer
H: Prayer room
I: Technical rooms
J: Storage room / Technical facilities

Ceiling plan

Glaring Lights

Dune Lights

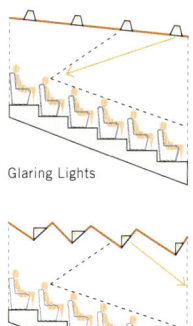

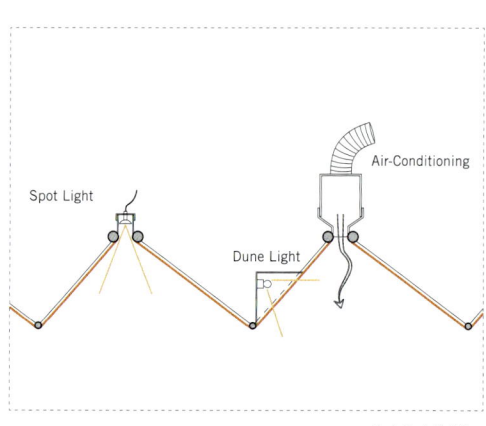

Detail of Lighting

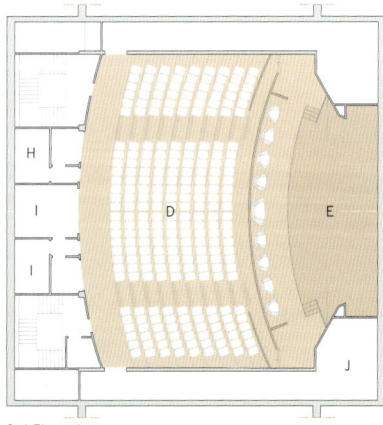

3rd Floor plan

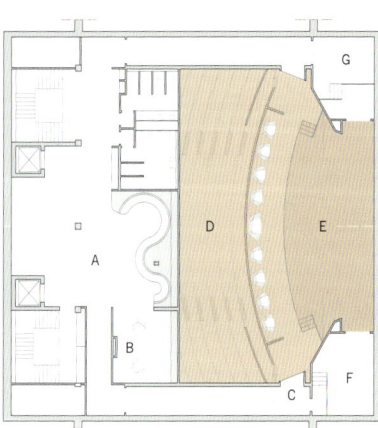

2nd Floor plan 1:500

Design firm: magma architecture
Designer: Martin Ostermann, Lena
Kleinheinz, Hendrik Bohle, Philipp
Mecke, Anke Noske, Carlos Lara
Consultant: Mechanical & Electrical
engineering- Sarraj SMEP Engineering
Consultants
Acoustics- Akustik Ingenieurbüro Moll
Total area: 820 m²
Contractor:
Main contractor, Fabric foyer, AC,
Electrical elements fitout- Décor,
Sharjah, UAE
Aluminium construction- Ellermann
GmbH, Rietberg, Germany
Client: Al Qasba Development Authority
Completion: Mar. 2012
Main materials: My Tx Stretch Color
(fabric), Substructure in aluminium
Site: Al Taawun Street, Sharjah, United
Arab Emirates

The renovation of the Masrah Al Qasba Theater was based
on the subtle atmospheric amalgamation of everyday life of
the past and the contemporary world of theatre. The client
also required a design rooted in the nature and history of the
Emirate of Sharjah as well as embracing its cultural future.
Back in nomadic days, news was transmitted orally in the
open-air of the desert landscape. The theater design refer-
ences Sharjah's nature and alludes to a fully enclosing sce-
nographic landscape. Undulating surfaces with light strips
on fold lines scatter across the ceiling and evoke scenes of
the evening sun streaking across sand dunes. Theater-goers
can disconnect from everyday life to immerse themselves in
the surprising and striking space of the staged narrative of
the theater.

The past and present are also reflected in the choice of
materials, and despite the high-tech, contemporary make
of the interior skin, it is created out of textile, a traditional
building material in the region. The textile wraps the walls
and ceiling of the 300-seat auditorium space in a continuous, smooth surface.

Lights on fold lines gently accentuate the double curvature
shapes, and they illuminate the space without blinding the
audience. Spotlights installed in the cracks in the surface
can be switched off to create dimmed illumination for
lectures and talks. On the other hand, the theatre lobby and
adjoining rooms feature a completely white space with soft
light in changing colors to create a space where visitors can
meet and linger.

地表の亀裂

Teruel-Zilla

Underground leisure lair and Public space / Teruel, Spain

Designer:
Mi5 arquitectos + PKMN
architectures

Article: Yasuhiko Taguchi
Photography: Miguel de
Guzmán and Javier de Paz

（上）Domingo Gasón 広場を北西側より見る

(Above) Plaza Domingo Gascón viewed
from the northwest

（上）メインエントランスまわり俯瞰

(Above) Looking down around the main entrance

（下）メインエントランスまわりを北東側より見る

(Bottom) Around the main entrance viewed from the northeast

（右上）メインエントランスまわり夕景

(Right above) Around the main entrance at twilight

（右下）サブエントランスまわり夜景

(Right bottom) Around the sub entrance at night

（上）下階のメザニンフロアより見る

(Above) Viewed from the lower level mezzanine

（右）クライミングジムがあるサブエントランス側の下階メザニンフロア

(Right) Lower level mezzanine with a climbing gym on the sub-entrance side

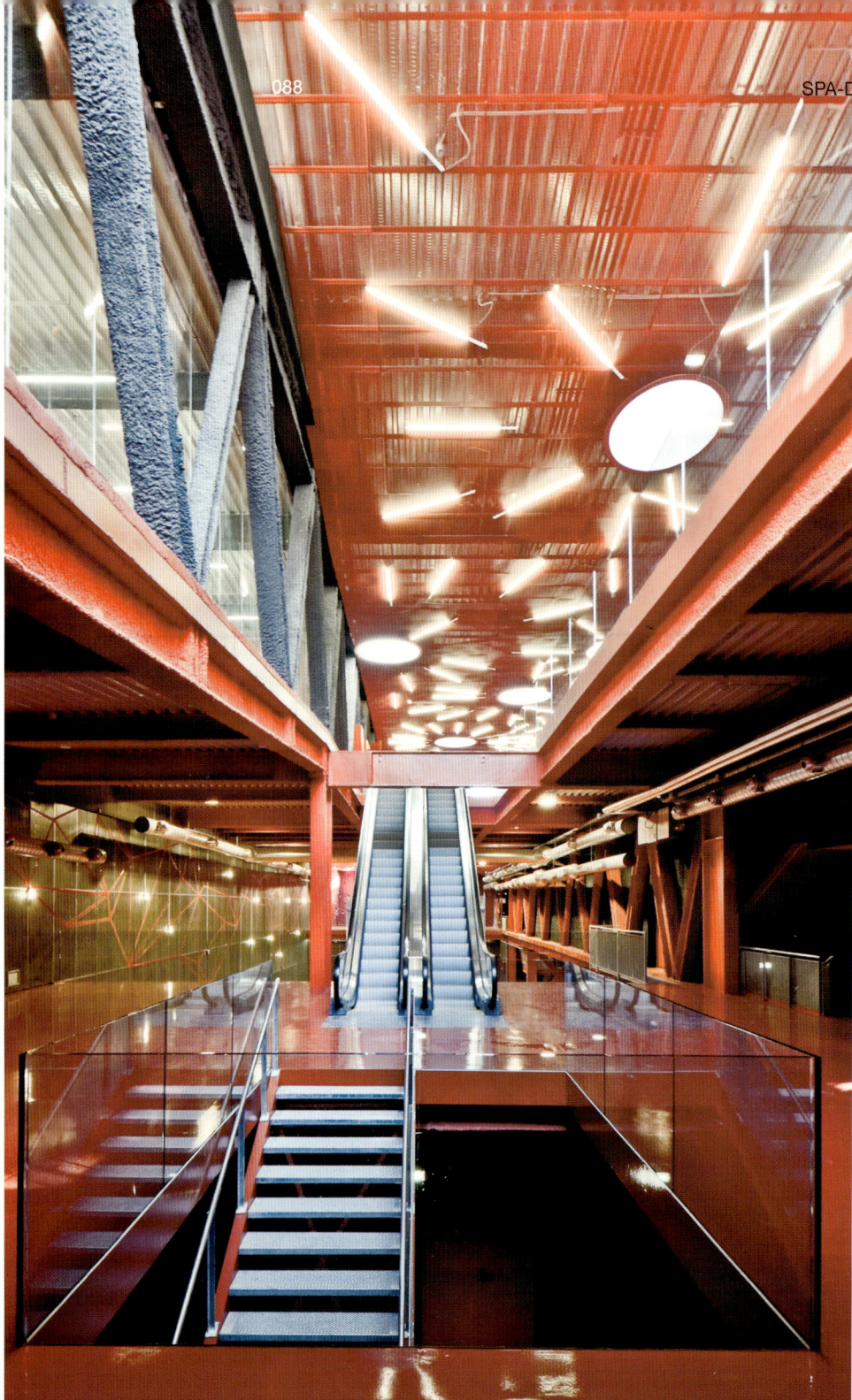

ここ、スペインのテルエル州のカルベは1987年に
イベリア半島で最初に恐竜が発見されたところで
ある。街には化石博物館があり、恐竜がテーマと
なり観光客を引きつける大きな要素となっている。
プロジェクトはこの街の"地下の魅力"をヒントに
したもので、街を活性化するコンセプトが作られた。
ドミンゴ・ガスコン広場の公共スペースは時代遅
れで、そこには古くなって使われないマーケットの
建物があった。プロジェクトは建物を取り壊し、
地下に若者のための大きなレジャー活動の施設
を作ることであった。
施設はテルエルの活動を育てる公共スペースとレ
ジャーセンターから成り、現代的イメージの大地
という要素と、ポップな表現として埋まった恐竜の
骨が使われた。デザインコンセプトは"地表の亀裂"
で、外へ押し出されて出来た新しい街の地形に地
下空間が創られた、というものである。地下に埋
め込まれ、構造物をカモフラージュしたこの方法
は古い街のセンターにある街並みを壊さずに大き
な公共施設を内部と外部に作ることを可能にした。
ここを訪れる人々にとって地上は広々とした公共
広場として、地下はさまざまな活動ができて、愉
しみがあり、スポーツに触れられる多目的の場に
変わった。
構造的な諸問題を解決し、建築的なプロトタイプ
を地下に作ることによって歴史地区の再開発と都
市生活を増強し、密度の高い公共施設を作るこ
とができた。このプロジェクトはテルエルのような
歴史が重要な要素となっている街に新たな開発の
方法を提示している。

（上）中央部吹き抜け

(Above) Open ceiling space at the central area

Here in the town of Galve in the Spanish province of Teruel,
the first dinosaur remains were found in the Iberian Pen-
insula in 1987. The town sports a fossil museum and the
dinosaur theme is a big element of attraction for tourists.
The project takes inspiration from the town's "underground
appeal" to revitalize the area.
The meager public space of Domingo Gascon Square was
dominated by an obsolete and underused market building.
The project decided to demolish the old structure and intro-
duce an underground facility for youth leisure activities.
The facility, which encompasses the leisure center and the
reclaimed old public square, aims to revitalize and to foster
the growth of Teruel and takes the form of a buried "Godzil-
la," a telluric element of contemporary and pop expression.
With this design concept, a big, buried volume pushes away

the ground and cracks it to produce a new urban topog-
raphy. Embedding and camouflaging allow the creation of
the interior and exterior of this large public facility without
disrupting the existing urban fabric of the city center.
Visitors can enjoy the surface which has turned into a public
square, and they can descend into the depths which have
become a multipurpose space and be entertained by meeting activities, fun, and sports.
Solving various structural issues and exploring architectural
prototypes that can revitalize the historical urban fabric
and revitalize city life, the project created an empower-
ing public facility. Moreover, it proposes a new method of
development for cities like Teruel which places high impor-
tance on its history.

（上）上階コリドール　　　　　（下）下階オーディトリアム

(Above) Upper level corridor　　(Bottom) Lower level auditorium

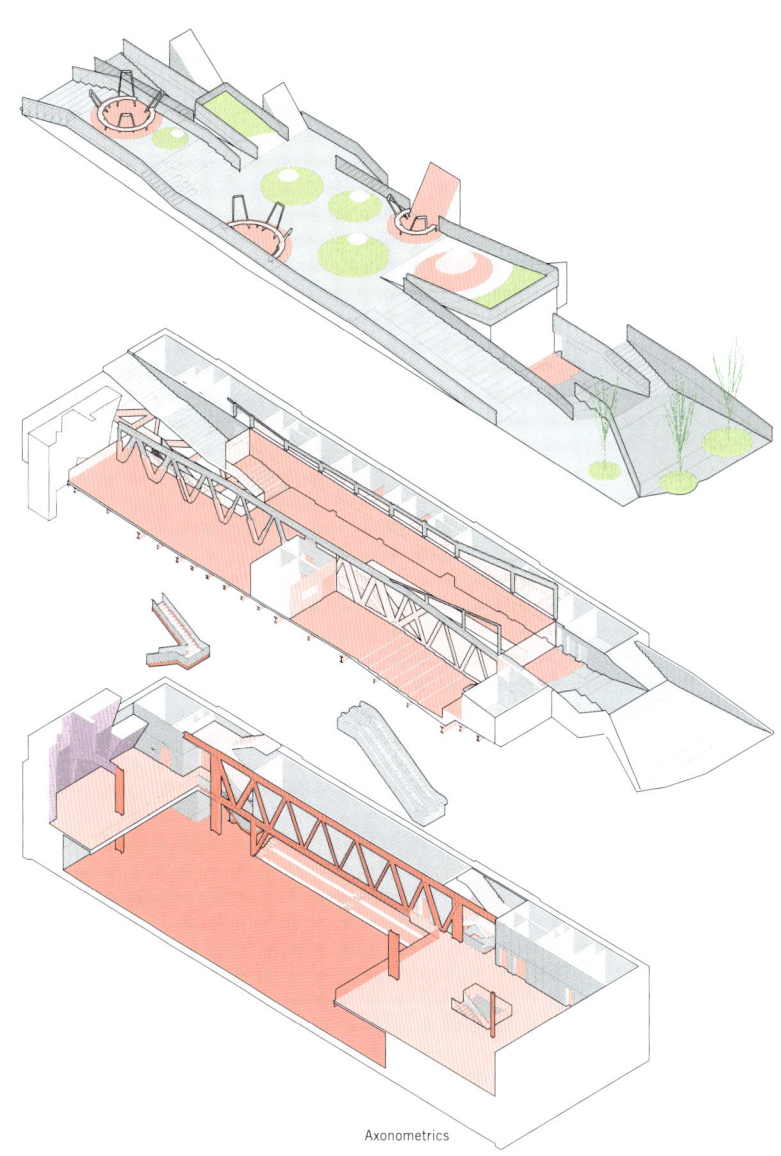

Axonometrics

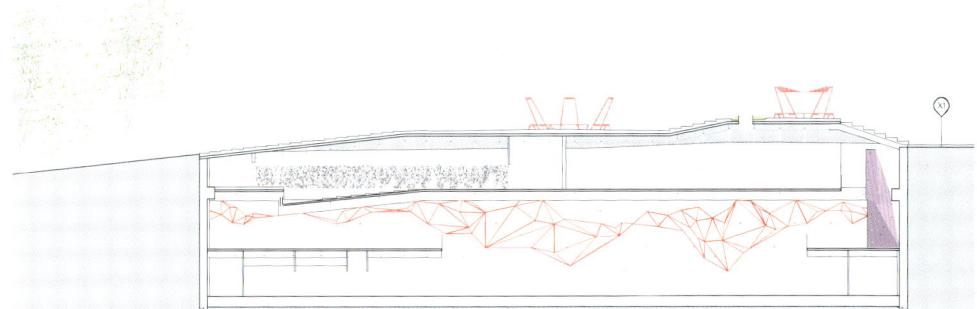

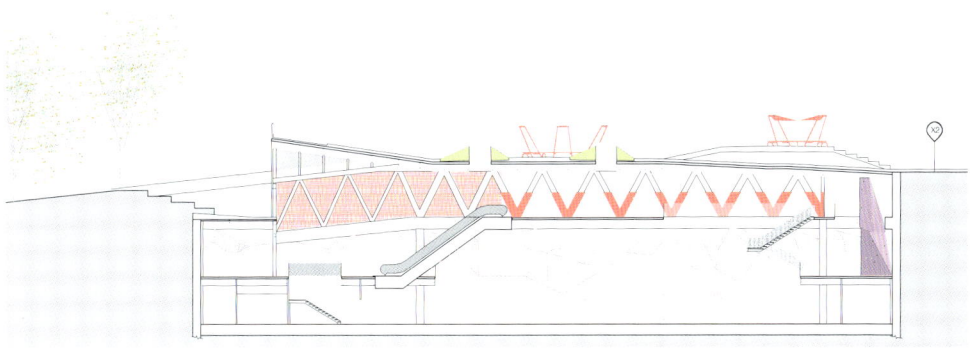

Section

Design firm: Mi5 arquitectos + PKMN [pac-man] architectures
Designer: Martin Ostermann, Lena Kleinheinz, Hendrik Bohle, Philipp Mecke, Anke Noske, Carlos Lara
Consultant: Urban Teruel, Teruel City Council Architectural Technologists/ María del Carmen Nombela and Ana Macipe
Structure engineering- Mecanismo Diseño y Cálculode Estructuras S.L.
Systems engineering- Solventa Ingenieros Consultores S.L.
Geotechnics- Geodeser S.A., Topography- Julia del Toro
Total area: Building work; 3.600 m² urbanization + 3005 m² built area
Contractor: Fomento de Construcciones y Contratas
Client: Urban Teruel, Teruel City Council
Construction phase: Nov. 2008–Dec. 2011
Main materials: Composite steel and concrete structure
Site: Plaza Domingo Gascón, Teruel, Spain

Designer: Serie Architects   Article: Yasuhiko Taguchi
Photography:
Edmund Sumner

London 2012
BMW Group
Pavilion

Temporary showroom / London

車のための
水上ステージ

ウォーターワークス川に浮かぶパビリオン

Pavilion floating on the Waterworks River

イギリス人はビクトリアン風の野外音楽ステージが大好きである。このアイデアをベースに、BMWグループパビリオンはBMW車の壮観な眺め、存在感、サービス、サスティナビリティーを表現することを求められた。パビリオンはオリンピックパークのウォーターワークス川に位置し、クラシックな演壇をイメージして作られた。細い柱で支えられた軽量の屋根をもつステージは建築を最小限にし、周囲の景観に溶け込んでいる。

柱のベースである床は水でおおわれ、その水がカスケード状に4面に流れ落ち、常にファサードに変化をもたらしている。この水の壁は上部にある繊細なパビリオンを支える水の演壇を形成している。床の水は反射のための浅いプールとなり、車、訪問客、オリンピック・サイト等、周囲の環境を映し出している。

パビリオンの各キャノピーの形はシンメトリーに作られた連続曲線カーブの使用で、静かさと合理性を形態で表している。

パビリオンは、ロンドンオリンピックの期間中BMWの新車のショーケースとして使われ、主に電機自動車などが展示された。終了後は他の場所に分散され、それぞれののセッテング中で再利用された。

Design firm: Serie Architects
Executive architects: Franken Architekten
Consultant:
Structural engineering- AKT II
Water feature specialist- Fountains Direct
MEP engineering- Atelier Ten
Project management- KSV Krüger
Schuberth Vandreike
Total area: 1,200 m²
Contractor: Nussli
Client: BMW (AG)
Completion: Jul. 2012
Main materials: Wall- Steel structure
with glazing, Flooring(roof)- The
GRP-lined reflecting pool,
Ceiling- Curved semi-monocoque timber
shell roofs supported by steel columns
Site: Olympic Park, London

（上）西側からの俯瞰

(Above) Overlooking the pavilion from
the west

（左）1階レベル（+9,600）

(Left) 1st floor level (+9,600)

（左上）南側コーナー外観

(Left above) Exterior view of the south corner

（右上）東側から見た全景ビリオン

(Left above) Whole exterior view from the east

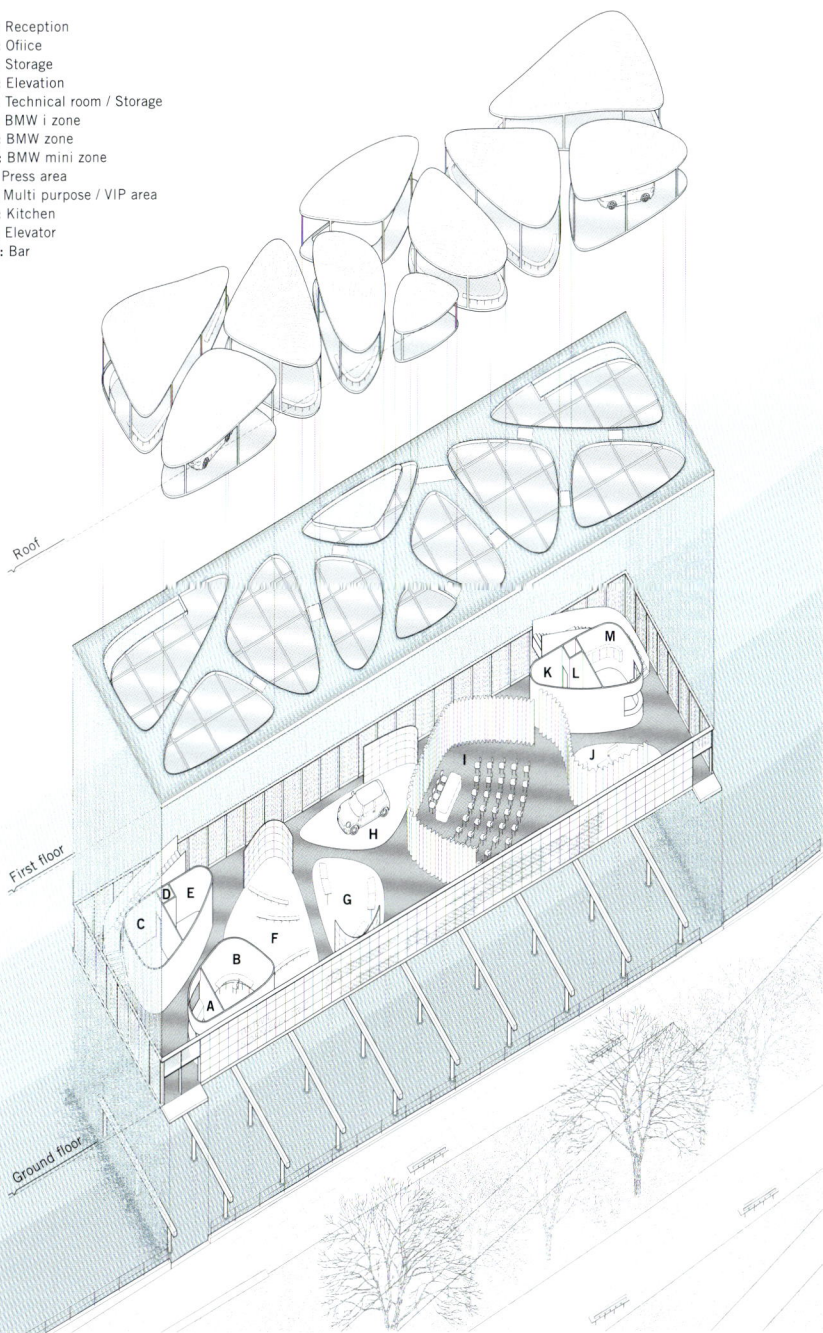

A: Reception
B: Ofiice
C: Storage
D: Elevation
E: Technical room / Storage
F: BMW i zone
G: BMW zone
H: BMW mini zone
I: Press area
J: Multi purpose / VIP area
K: Kitchen
L: Elevator
M: Bar

Axonometric 1:600

The British are particularly fond of the Victorian bandstand. Based on this concept, the BMW Group Pavilion addressed questions of spectacle and presence, of the product and service offering, and of sustainability.

The pavilion is positioned directly on the Waterworks River in the Olympic Park and its design re-imagines the classical podium. The thin columns supporting the stage with the lightweight roofs minimize the architecture and blend in with the surroundings. The first floor that forms the plinth is covered with water, and this water spills down on all four sides of the pavilion, creating a constantly changing façade. This wall of water forms a "liquid podium" supporting the delicate pavilions above it. Moreover, the surface of the first floor is a shallow pool that reflects its surroundings, including the cars, the visitors, and the Olympic site.

The shape of the pavilion roofs emanates a similar calm and rational attitude to geometry through the use of off-phase and symmetrically set sinusoidal curves. One of the pavilion's functions is to display BMW's new fleet of electric and hybrid vehicles. At the end of the Games, these pavilions were dispersed to other locations, with each pavilion finding a new home within a natural setting.

Contemporary Art Museum (CAM) Raleigh

Museum / Raleigh, North Carolina

Designer:
Lawrence Scarpa

Article: Yasuhiko Taguchi
Photography:
John Edward Linden,
Nick Pironio and Lawrence
Scarpa

（右・下）エントランスまわり夕景

(Right, bottom) View of the entrance
at twilight

アートワーク としての キャノピー

新設されたキャノピー
Extended new canopy

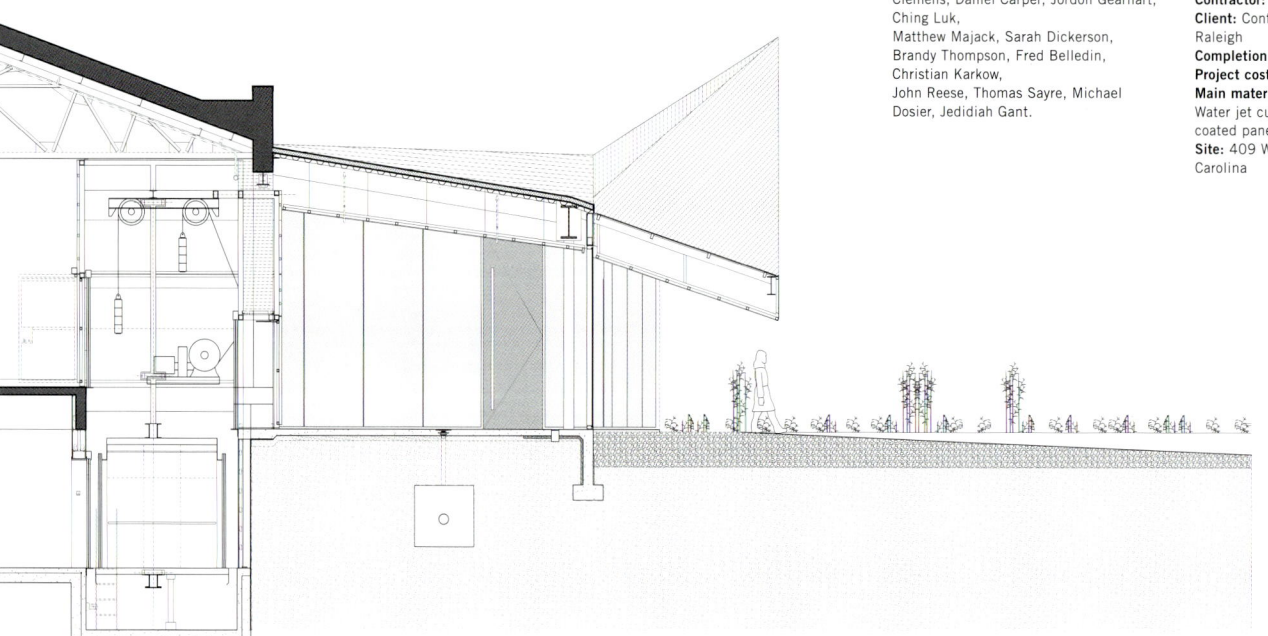

（上）メインギャラリーとストリートギャラ
リーを隔てる吹き抜け

(Above) Open ceiling space separating
the main gallery from the Street Gallery

Design firm: Brooks Scarpa/Clearscapes
Designer: Lawrence Scarpa, Steve
Schuster
Mark Buckland and Jon Zellweger- Proj-
ect architects,
Angela Brooks, Brad Buter, Silke
Clemens, Daniel Carper, Jordon Gearhart,
Ching Luk,
Matthew Majack, Sarah Dickerson,
Brandy Thompson, Fred Belledin,
Christian Karkow,
John Reese, Thomas Sayre, Michael
Dosier, Jedidiah Gant.

Consultant: Lysaght & Associates, PA-
Structural engineering,
The Wooten Company- Mechanical
electrical plumbing engineering
Total area: 2071.7 m² (83.6 m² new
entry lobby)
Contractor: CT Wilson Construction
Client: Contemporary Art Museum
Raleigh
Completion: 2011
Project cost: $5,800,000
Main materials: Polycarbonate panels,
Water jet cut perforated aluminum zinc
coated panels
Site: 409 W. Martin St., Raleigh, North
Carolina

Section at entry pavilion 1:150

（上）地階ギャラリーから吹き抜けを見上
げる

(Above) Looking up at the open ceiling
space from the gallery on the basement

ノース・カロライナの州都ラリーに古い鉄道駅の
ある歴史的開発地区がある。コンテンポラリーアー
トミュージアムCAMはこの地区にある、昔鉄工所
や倉庫として使われた由緒ある2層の建物を改装
してオープンした。

歴史ある建物をリノベーションすることによって、
CAMはこの街の大切な遺産を保存し、サスティナ
ビリティーと歴史保存のリーダーであることをアピー
ルしている。

既存のレンガ建物に90㎡の玄関キャノピーが新し
く付けられた。ロビーは折れたパネルでドラマチッ
クに構成されたキャノピーの下に作られ、ガラス
で囲まれている。キャノピーの大胆な形状はアメリ
カ南部で力強いシンボルとして使われているマグノ
リアの木の種からインスピレーションが取られた。
花びらのパターンは穴空きアルミ シートで作られ、
一つのフォルムの繰り返しで三つのサイズから成り、
ポリカーボネイト パネルに付けられている。パター
ンはランダムに配置されたのではなく、場所により
十分光が透過するように計画された。

メインギャラリーは露出したオリジナルのスチール・
トラストと丸窓があり、天井の高いドラマチックな
スペースとなった。このギャラリーは500人が収
容できる各種イベント会場にもなり、隣には細長
い吹き抜けをはさんで2番目のギャラリーStreet
Gallaryがある。このギャラリーはガラスとスチー
ルのブリッジで結ばれ、上部から下のギャラリー
が見下せるようにデザインされた。

The Historic Depot District in Raleigh, the capital of North
Carolina, went under revitalization. Located in this district
is a historic two-story building that saw previous life as a
metal works and warehouse, and has lately become the new
home of Raleigh's Contemporary Art Museum (CAM).
By repurposing this important building, CAM preserves an
important part of Raleigh's history and demonstrates its
commitment to sustainability and leadership in historic
preservation.
To the existing structure was added a new 90 square-meter
entrance canopy structure. The lobby is a glass-enclosed
space set beneath a dramatic folded-panel roof. The canopy's bold shape was inspired by the seed of the magnolia
tree, a powerful symbol of the American South. The flower
petal pattern was created from punched aluminum sheets,
with a repetition of forms creating three different sizes, and
attached to polycarbonate panels. The patterns were not
placed randomly, but planned so enough light would shine
through in certain places.
The Main Gallery is a dramatic space with tall ceilings, the
original metal trusses exposed, and with a row of porthole-
like features. This gallery can accommodate some 500
people for a variety of events. A second gallery, the Street
Gallery, is located next door but separated by an open
trench in the concrete floor. The Street Gallery is accessible
by a glass and metal bridge spanning the trench, providing
views down into the third gallery below.

A: Patio
B: Entry pavilion
C: Main gallery
D: Open to below
E: Street gallery
F: WC
G: Parking

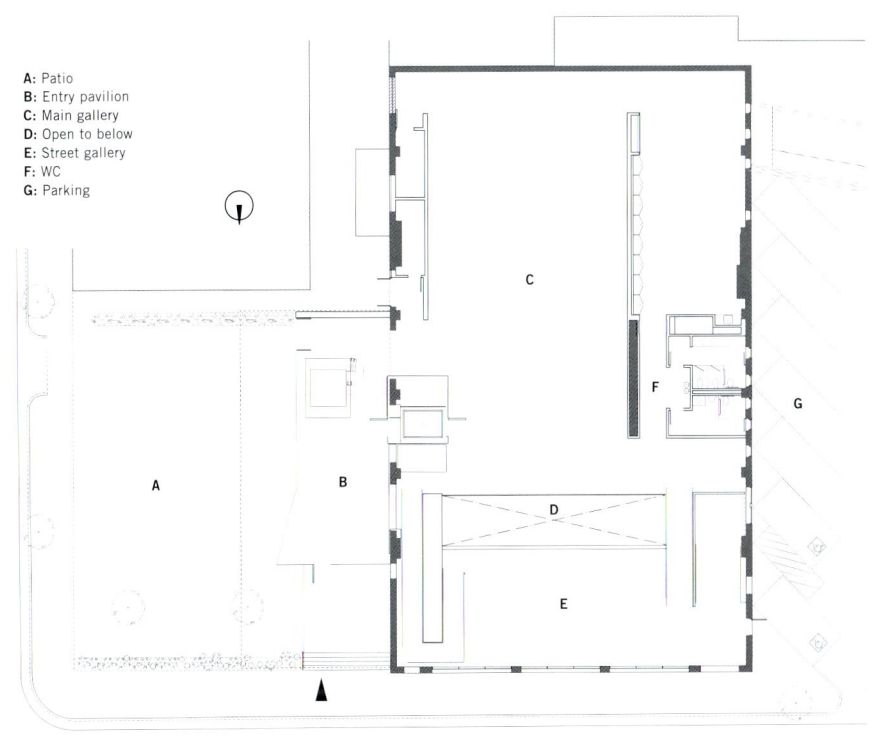

Ground floor plan 1:500

A Cantina

Cafeteria & Museum shop / Santiago de Compostela

Designer:
Estudio Nômad

Article: Yasuhiko Taguchi
Photography: BISimages/
Héctor Santos-Díez

ミュージアムショップ側から見たカフェテ
リア

Cafeteria viewed from the museum shop

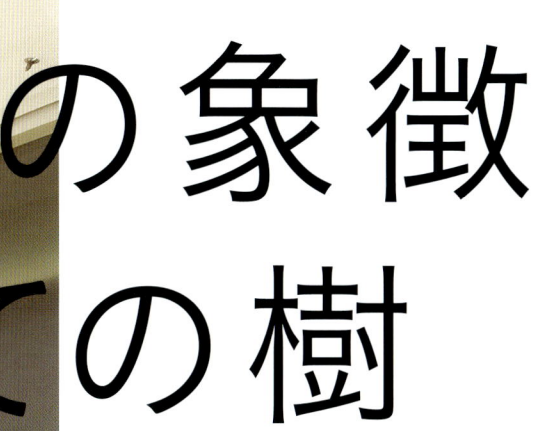

祝祭の象徴としての樹

スペインのカソリックの聖地として知られるサンティアゴ・デ・コンポステーラにあるガリシア公文書館に、カフェテリアとミュージアムショップが作られた。建築家は既存の建物を改修し、ガリシア文化のアイデンティティーが感じられるコンテンポラリーな提案をした。

各スペースを分離していた厚い壁に二つの穴を開け、このトンネルを介して二つのスペースを作り、この地区の伝統的な食堂からヒントを得て、カフェテリアとショップが同時に使用、運営できるようなコンセプトを立てた。カフェテリアでは二つの長いテーブルが並列に配置され、各テーブルには小屋の面影を持ち、地元で人気のある祭りを感じさせる簡素化した樹が取り付けられた。壁に沿って置かれた長いカウンターはカフェテリアとショップを統合し、ウエイターステーションの役目を果たしている。カウンターの腰は幾何学的パターンが奔放なカラーで描かれ、ガリシアの伝統的フォークアートのデモンストレーションとして無地の空間に鮮やかさを作り出している。カフェテリアのサポート施設は白い円筒形の囲いの中にあり、軽飲食用のサービス・キッチンとしてデザインされた。

ミュージアムショップは、調整棚付きの異なるサイズと高さをもった本棚とカウンターが多様性を生かすようにランダムに配置された。

市の文化施設を特色づけている複雑さにもかかわらず、このデザインは全体のプロジェクトに影響を与えることなく異なった要素からなる家具で構成され、色彩と木の質感によって全体の雰囲気を豊かにしている。

（左）ウエイターステーションの機能を持
たせたロングカウンター

(Left) Long counter functioning as a
waiter station

（下）ミュージアムショップの高さ調整が
できる本棚

(Bottom) Height-adjustable bookshelves
in the museum shop

Situated in the Catholic holy site of Santiago de Compostela in Galicia, Spain, the designer created a cafeteria and museum store within the Archive of Galicia. The team renovated the existing building, and they proposed a contemporary design that alludes to the Galician cultural identity.

The design concept connects the two areas through two separate holes drilled in the thick wall that separates each space while still maintaining spatial distinction. This allows the spaces to be used and managed separately and simultaneously as traditionally seen in cafeterias at Galician villages. The designer interprets the cafeteria as a model of traditional establishment in Galicia. The elongated tables are arranged in parallel under schematic trees which evoke popular festivities being held in their shadows. A long counter that runs through the wall unifies and serves both the cafeteria and the museum shop. Above, traditional Galician folk art is interpreted through geometric patterns and bright colors. Supporting the cafeteria and bar area, a round and rotund space provides a secluded kitchen area to prepare food.

At the museum shop, adjustable bookshelves and counters of different dimensions and heights are distributed randomly, allowing versatility.

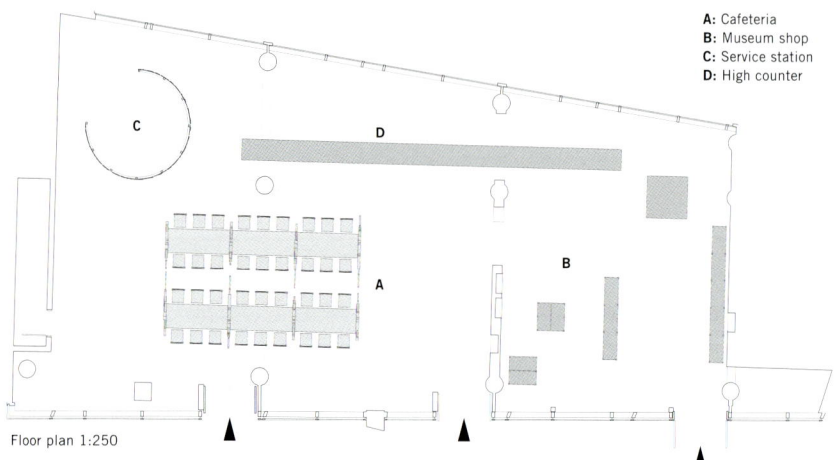

A: Cafeteria
B: Museum shop
C: Service station
D: High counter

Floor plan 1:250

Despite the complicated character of the complex, this design consists of different elements of furniture, without affecting the general project. These elements enrich the overall project through the qualities of color and wood, providing character and accommodating various types of activities.

Design firm: Estudio Nômad
Designer: José-Antonio Vázquez-Martín (Architect), Enrique de Santiago (Interior designer), Beatriz Asorey (Draughtswoman.)
Total area: 277 m²
Contractor: Furniture manufacturer- BMC, Lighting manufacturer- Iguzzini
Client: Fundación Cidade da Cultura de Galicia
Completion: Oct. 2010
Main materials: Oak wood, Corian, Royal Mosa tiles
Site: Monte Gaiás S/N 15702, City Santiago de Compostela, Spain

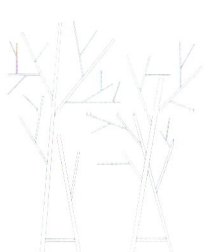

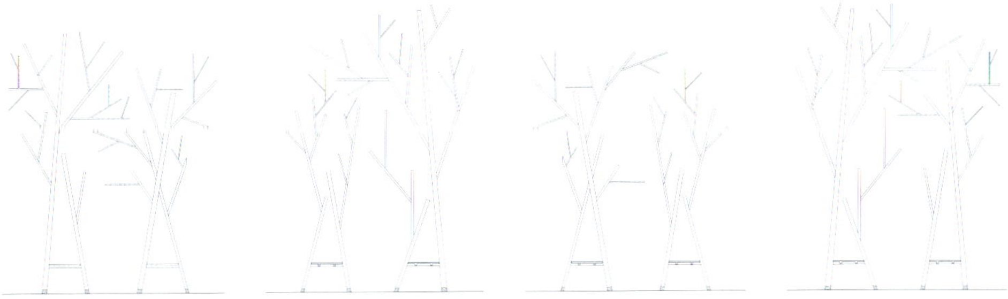

Elevation 1:200

（上）ミュージアムショップからカフェテリア方向を見る

(Above) View towards the cafeteria from the museum shop

（右）厚い壁に開けられた二つの穴

(Right) Two holes drilled in the thick wall

スピードの形態

Nike
Camp Victory

Temporary showcase / Eugene, Oregon

Designer:
Skylab Architecture

Article: Yasuhiko Taguchi
Photography:
Photography Boone Speed
for Skylab Architecture

（左頁上）キャンプ・ヴィクトリー鳥瞰

(Left page above) Bird's eye view of the
Camp Victory

（上）キャンプ・ヴィクトリー全景

(Above) Whole view of the Camp Victory

スピードトンネル・パビリオンの舳先
Bow of the Speed Tunnel pavilion

FIND YOUR GREATNESS.

左 スピードトンネル・パビリオンと右
NIKE+パビリオン
Left; Speed Tunnel pavilion and Right;
NIKE+pavilion

キャンプ・ビクトリーは2012年の米国オリンピック陸上予選大会の間、ナイキのイノベーションのショーケースとして作られた。三つのパビリオンから成る展示場はオレゴン大学の陸上競技場に10ヵ月間仮設された。

パビリオンの断面形状は短距離走者がスタートブロックから飛び出てきた時のような、上体を曲げたカンティレバー状で、構造上ぎりぎりまで引き伸ばしたフォルムになっている。このフォルムは3層の高さのスチールフレーム構造で、軽量の半透明ポリエステル膜によって包まれている。交差している

トラック競技の走路は空間を開いたり、再びすぼめたりした幾何形体でパビリオン同士を結びつけている。

このプロジェクトのコンセプトはいかにランニングをビジュアル化するかに焦点が当てられた。3次元のモデリングとモーショングラフィックは、反復プロセスを通して実現したストラクチャー、デジタルメディア、商品ディスプレイを統合させることを可能にした。

各々139㎡から成る三つのインタラクティブ・パビリオンは経済的な方法で作られ、ナイキ商品の

精神を表している。Speed Tunnelの展示はLEDスクリーンに絶え間なく映し出されたリアルタイムの選手をトレースしている。Shoe Labはナイキの二つの新しい靴のテクノロジーを展示し、NIKE+は距離とスピードを記録するトレッドミルで走るゲームを通して、ボード上のリーダーと競争するゲームになっている。

試合後パビリオンは解体され、元のサッカー場に戻った。

（左）スピードトンネル・パビリオンのエントランス

(Left) Entrance of the Speed Tunnel pavilion

（下）スピードトンネル・パビリオンの展示

(Bottom) Display of the Speed Tunnel pavilion

（左）シューラボ・パビリオンの展示

(Left) Display in the Shoe Lab pavilion

（右）NIKE+パビリオンのトレッドミル・ゲーム

(Right) Treadmill game in the NIKE+pavilion

Design firm: Skylab Architecture
Designer: Jeff Kovel- Design principal, Sebastian Guivernau- Project architect, Brent Grubb- Project manager, Claran Fitzgerald, Lizzie Falkenstein- Project team
Consultant:
Hush Studios- Digital media, Big Giant- Graphic design
FTL Design Engineering Studio- Event design engineering,
PAE Consulting Engineers- Mechanical engineering
Skylab Architecture- Pavilion interior design, Birdair Inc.- Pavilion contractor
Tangram International Exhibitions Inc.- Interior contractor,
Noel Lesley Event Services Inc.- Event services
Total area: 6,280 m²
Contractor: Hiraoka & Co. LTD. (Pavilion fabric)
Client: Nike Inc.
Period: Jun. 22–Jul. 1, 2012
Main materials: Lightweight steel structure, Fabric
Site: Hayward Field, University of Oregon, Eugene, Oregon

Speed Tunnel plan

Nike + plan

Shoe Lab plan

Camp Victory was built as a showcase of Nike innovation during the 2012 U.S. Olympic Trials Track & Field Competition. A series of three pavilions were installed for ten days at the University of Oregon's sports field.

Like a sprinter coming out of the starting blocks, the pavilions lean and cantilever, stretching to their structural physical limits. The three-story, steel-framed pavilions are sheathed in a light-weight, translucent polymer membrane. Intersecting running lanes connect the pavilions, unfolding and refolding the space.

The project design was inspired by the visualization of speed. Three-dimensional modeling and motion graphics allowed for a synthesis of the structure, media, and product displays that was realized through an iterative process.

The three interactive pavilions are each 139 square-meters, expressing the spirit of Nike products built on an economy of means. The Speed Tunnel exhibit tracked in real-time athletes in motion displayed on a continuous LED-screened wall. The Shoe Lab featured two new Nike footwear technologies, and NIKE+ connected runners through a game of human-powered treadmills recording distance and speed to

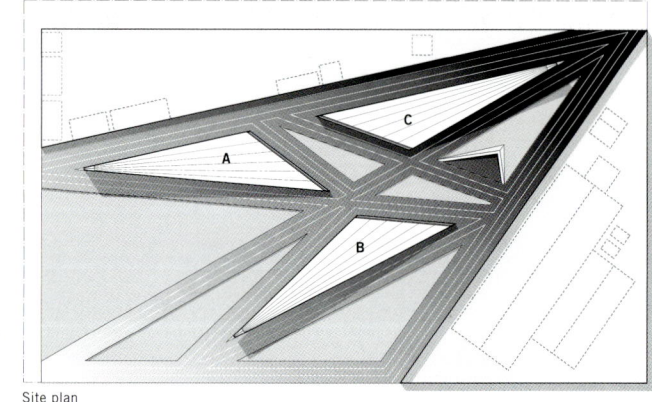

A: Speed Tunnel
B: Nike +
C: Shoe Lab

Site plan

compete for the leader board.

At the end of the Olympic Trials, the structures were disassembled, and the location returned to its regular function as a soccer field.

ランタンの
ショーケース

Aesop Installation
at I.T Hysan One

Designer:
Cheungvogl Architects

Article: Ikunori Ara
Photography: Cheungvogl
Architects

Installation / Hong Kong

（上）ウインドーディスプレイを見る

(Above) View of the window display

香港の建築設計事務所Cheungvoglはこれまで、オーストラリアのスキンケアブランドAesopのためにいくつかのユニークなインスタレーションやショップデザインをアジアやヨーロッパで行っている。この空間デザインは期間限定のインスタレーションである。

デザインは、伝統的な白と黒のたくさんのランタンが宙に浮かんでいるイメージからインスパイアされた。ディスプレイ棚の代わりに800個の半透明のリシンボックスを高さの異なるスチールロッドの上部に取り付け、手前から奥へとだんだん高く配置してランタンのタワーのように形づくっている。

デザイナーは「ボックスは自然に増殖しているようであり、見えない糸で吊るされているかのようでもある」と言っている。これらランタンは通り側だけに開口部を設けた半透明のファブリックに囲われ、デリケートな色のない清浄な明かりを周囲にふりまいている。いくつかのボックスには "Aesop" の商品が展示され、他のいくつかのボックスには思いもかけない音、香り、感触を潜ませている。Aesopのコンサルタントのために、仮のサービスカウンター設けられたが、このインスタレーションは2週間後には解体され、より常設的なカウンターが同じビル内につくられた。

（上上）メイン展示エリア見上げ

(Above above) Looking up at the main
exhibition area

（上下）メイン展示エリア正面

(Above bottom) Front view of the main
exhibition area

Honk Kong Architects Cheungvogl has created many unique
installations and stores across Asia and Europe for the
Australian skincare brand Aesop that is renowned for the
unusual display of its products. For the design the architects were inspired by black and white images of hundreds
of traditional floating lanterns. Thus instead of display
shelves the installation used eight hundred translucent
resin boxes arranged on top of steel rods of varying heights.
With the taller rods positioned towards the back the boxes
appear to be stacked like a tower of lanterns. As the architects state 'each box is ascending at its own pace, as if

being drawn up by an invisible thread'. A translucent fabric
enclosed the installation with only one side being open to
the street, which along with the delicate, low lighting and
monochrome colouring created an intimate atmosphere. In
some boxes Aesop products were displayed and in others
creating an element of surprise there were unexpected
sounds, scent and touch. The installation also served as a
counter for Aesop consultants to operate from. After two
weeks the installation was dismantled and a more perma-
nent counter was constructed in the same building.

（上）メイン展示エリア側面

(Above) Side view of the main exhibition area

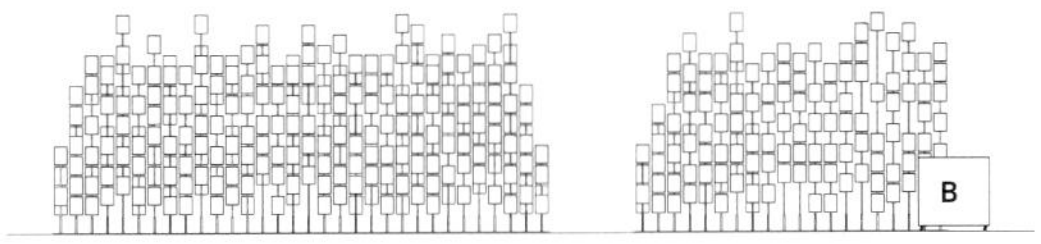

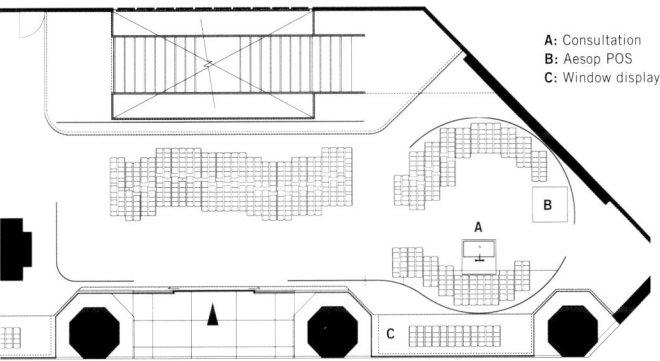

Elevation

A: Consultation
B: Aesop POS
C: Window display

Floor plan 1.200

Designer: Cheungvogl Architects
Client: Aesop
Total area: 100 m²
Completion: Dec. 2011
Main materials: Translucent resin boxes with steel rods
Site: I.T, Hysan One, Causeway Bay, Hong Kong

SPA-DE Vol.19

Raiffeisen's flagship branch

Bank / Zurich

Designer:
NAU together with Drexler
Guinand Jauslin Architekten

Article: Yasuhiko Taguchi
Photography: Jan Bitte

現代の肖像画

（下）外観

(Bottom) Exterior view

（下）カスタマーホール
(Bottom) Customer hall

チューリッヒのクロイツ広場にあるライファイセン銀行のフラッグシップ店は、顧客と従業員の間にある旧来の障害物を取り除き、銀行を人びとが出合う空間に変えた。

最先端の技術は銀行の必要設備の多くを隠し、コンピューターの端末は家具の中に取り込まれた。ロボットによる取り出しシステムは24時間利用できるセーフティボックスへのアクセスを可能にし、新しいタイプの銀行が作られた。銀行のスペースは従来の銀行のイメージと異なり、明るくラグジュアリーで、まるで最先端の商業施設のようにデザインされた。顧客はテーブルに取り付けられたタッ

チスクリーンで最新の株相場や銀行のサービスを検索したり、あるいは相談用の会議室へ簡単に移動することができる。

顧客と従業員のエリアにある境界は、なめらかな流れるような白壁によって変化がつけられた。このグラフィカルな人造大理石の壁は、最新のデジタル技術によってドリルされて作られた。モチーフはこの地域のよく知られた歴史的人物像をデジタル処理した抽象的イメージである。この壁のイメージは銀行が地域の文化的遺産に根付いていることを示すとともに、将来に向けた姿勢を表している。

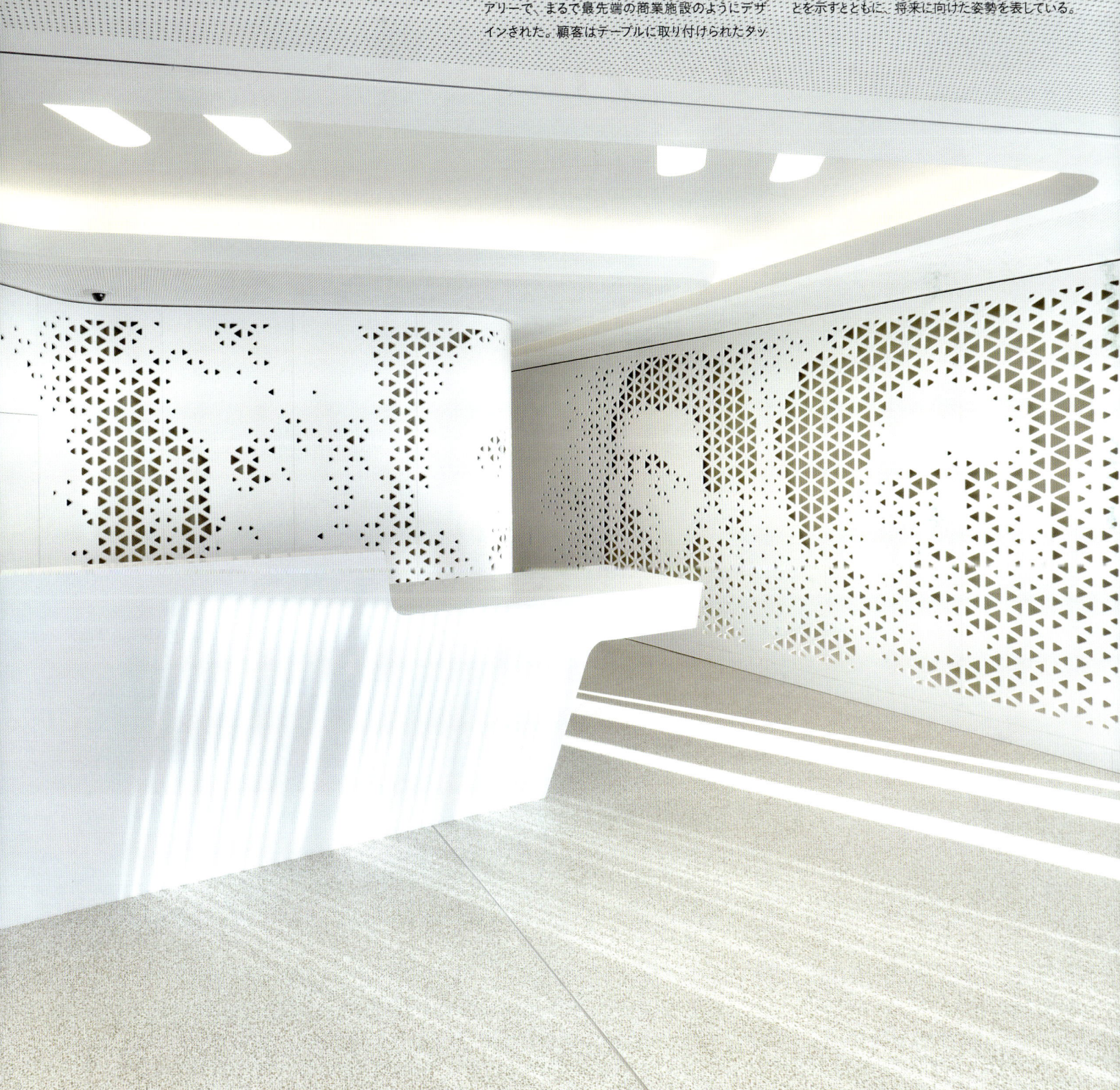

（上）ラウンジ側からカスタマーホールを
通して入り口方向見返し

(Above) Looking back at the entrance
from the lounge side through the customer hall

（右）店内エントランス付近からラウンジ
方向を見る

(Right) View towards the lounge area
from the entrance side

（上）オフィスエリア

(Above) Office area

（右）内照式グラフィックウオールのディ
テール

(Right) Detail of the graphical wall with
backup lighting

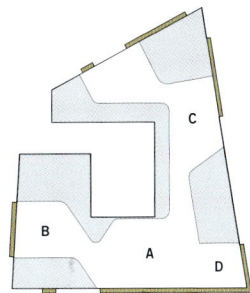

Floor plan

A: Customer hall
B: Lounge
C: Office
D: 24H

Panel Detial 1:15

Design firm: NAU together with Drexler
Guinand Jauslin Architekten
Consultant:
Site supervision- Archobau AG,
Mechanical- PGMM Switzerland AG,
Electrical- Mosimann & Partner AG,
Lighting- Sommerlatte & Sommerlatte,
Wall pattern- ROK, Rippmann Oesterle &
Knaus,
Interactive design- i-art interactive,
Acoustics- Braune & Roth
Total area: 400 m²

Contractor:
Walls covering & furniture- Glaeser
Baden AG, Glasing- Blaser Baden AG,
Plaster- Salvini AG, Flooring- Walo,
Electrical- Gebr. Bräm AG,
Ventilation and Cooling- Max Keller AG,
Heating- Amman & Schmid AG,
Painting- Ziebold,
Security- Gunnebo, Securiton, Loose
Furniture- Wohnbedarf
Client: Raiffeisen Bank Switzerland
Completion: Jun. 2011
Main materials: Terrazzo, Carpet,
Gypsum panels, Fabric
Site: Zeltweg 93, Zurich

Raiffeisen's flagship bank branch located in Zurich's Kreuz-
platz dissolves the traditional barriers between customer and
employee, turning the bank into a space where people meet.
Advanced technologies make the banking infrastructure
mostly invisible, and computer terminals have been con-
cealed in the furniture elements. A robotic retrieval system
grants 24-hour access to safety deposit boxes, creating a
new type of banking experience.
Unlike a traditional bank interior, the space is light with
an exclusive feel, and it is closer to a high-end retail environment. Customers can check the latest stock quotes or
access banking services on a touch screen-equipped table,
or move to meeting rooms for private discussions.
The boundary between client and employee areas is articu-
lated by smoothly flowing, white walls. These graphical,
manmade marble walls were produced using advanced
digital production techniques and show abstract images of
some of the area's most important historical figures. The
murals serve to connect the bank to the region's cultural
history, while looking clearly towards the future.

Casanueva's Pharmacy

Pharmacy / Murcia, Spain

Designer: Clavel Arquitectos　Article: Yasuhiko Taguchi
Photography: David Frutos

プレハブ什器の構成美

（上）ファサード夜景

(Above) Facade at night

（右）北側見た外観

(Right) Exterior viewed from the north

店内右側より入り口方向を見る

View towards the entrance from the
right side in the store

（上）入り口より店内を見る

(Above) Looking into the store from the entrance

（左）販売カウンターを通して調剤室方向を見る

(Left) View towards the laboratory through the sales counter

スペインでは近年薬局の規則変更もあって、健康に対する新しいサービスやそれに伴う魅力ある売り場デザインが求められるようになってきた。この店もそんな一つ。

店頭部に吹き抜けを持つ2層のこの店の改装は2ヵ月間の短期間で、最初の1ヵ月間は販売を続けながら工事をしなければならなかった。そのため多くの建築的要素はプレハブにする必要があった。

店は比較的地味な地域にあり、ストアフロントは2層分の高さのFARMACIA(薬局の意)のロゴで立体的にデザインされた。サインは薬局としてのアイデンティティーだけではなく、西側からの強い日差しを避けるために用いられている。夜になると照明で遠方からの視認性を高め、近づくとその大きさから抽象的なグラフィックとなっている。店内は天井から壁を通って床までグリーンのメタルパネルで包まれ、床は同色のエポキシ樹脂塗装で処理されている。ディスプレイ棚はグリーンを背景に内部照明された光沢のある白で、5段の面があり、浮いたようにデザインされ、店内の用途の異なったエリアを分割している。このディスプレイシステムは回転するデスク、椅子、展示台と展示棚から構成されている。

天井、壁に使用したメタルパネルが工場生産であるのはもちろん、ファサードのサインとディスプレイ棚等、全ての家具もワークショップで作られた。

（右）店内奥からウインドー側を見る
(Right) View towards the window from
the inner side of the store

In recent years, changes to rules and regulations for pharmacies in Spain have led to a new approach in sales, including new health services and new sales floor designs. This shop is representative of this change.

The renovation of the two-story store with a double-height façade was completed in just two months, made more difficult in the first month because sales needed to continue during the construction. Due to this complexity, prefabricating as many architectural elements as possible was necessary. Located in a relatively plain neighborhood, the storefront was designed as a double-height window with a 3-D "FARMACIA" logo. This not only functions as the drugstore's identity, but also provides shade from the strong, western sunlight. The sign, which lights up at night, can only be discerned from a certain distance, turning into illegible, abstract shapes when approaching it.

Inside the shop, a green, metallic cladding descends from the ceiling through the back wall down to the floor, the latter of which is coated with an epoxy-resin of the same color. These serve as a background for the display shelves, which are self-illuminated, glossy-white tubular elements in five levels that seem to float and divide the space into different areas. They also make up a rotating desk, a seat, a pulpit, and display shelves.

In order to keep to the strict deadline, the façade and all the furniture were prefabricated in a workshop, including the slat cladding.

A: Sales area
B: Rotating desk
C: Laboratory
D: WC
E: Office

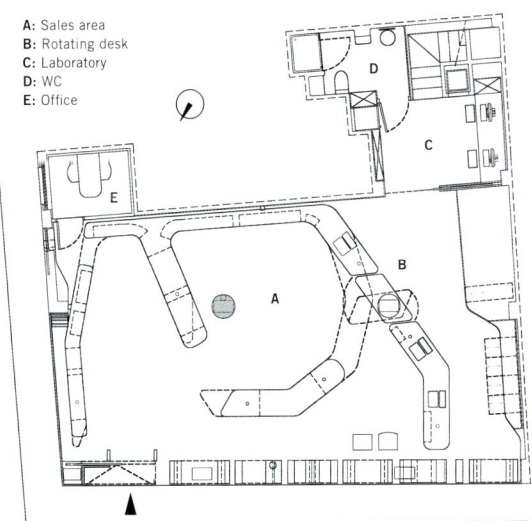

Floor plan 1:200

Design firm: Clavel Arquitectos
Designer: Manuel Clavel Rojo
Collaborators: Robin Harloff, Mauricio Méndez, David Hernández
Total area: 180.18 m²
Client: Ms. Alicia Casanueva and Mr. Francisco Lomo
Completion: Sep. 2010
Main materials: Steel (furniture and types), Painted aluminium (metallic slat cladding), Epoxy-resin (pavement) and Glass
Site: Cartagena Street 71, Murcia, Spain

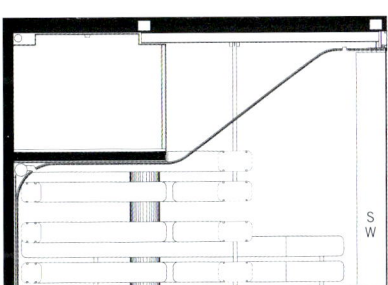

Section 1:150

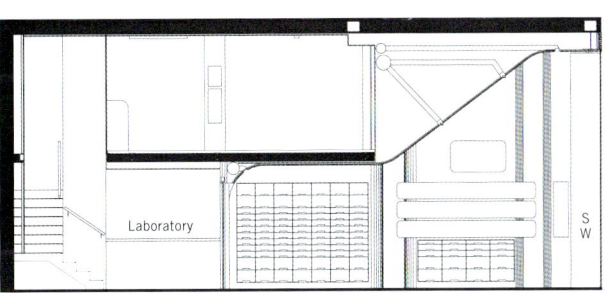

Edgecliff Medical Centre

Medical Centre / Edgecliff, Australia

Designer:
NAU together with Drexler
Guinand Jauslin Architekten

Article: Yasuhiko Taguchi
Photography: Jan Bitte

柔らかな
空間

（左頁・上）レセプションブース

(Left page, above) Reception booth

（左）入り口よりレセプションブースを見る

(Left) Reception booth viewed from the entrance

Design firm: Enter Architecture
Designer: Patrick Keane
Design team: Johanna Doerfel
Total area: 150 m²
Contractor: William Keeler
Carpentry: Chris Lain Construction
Internal finishes: Robert Makenzie
Lighting: Will Electric
Architectural assistant: Noor El-Gewely,
Derick Uong, David Kirkland

Client: Annabel Stuckey, Minnd
Foundation
Completion: Aug. 2012
Main materials: Floor- Existing concrete
floor polished, Wall- Laser-cut MDF
sheets,
Ceiling- Laser-cut MDF sheets,
Furniture- Fixed timber seating, inbuilt
planters
Site: Edgecliff, NSW 2027, Australia

ここは医療センター内に新しく出来た、自閉症児に特化した部局である。150㎡と控えめな広さで、中央に壁と一体となったレセプションカウンターを配し、周りに診察室を三つ、倉庫を一つ配した。2階は子供が自由に遊べる空間である。

カウンターを中心核に、それを取り囲むパーティション壁に呼応するボリュームある垂れ壁や梁が波のようにうねり、3次曲線を描く。ところどころに据えられた曲線のルーバーが柔らかいラインを描く。循環するラインやアールは人々に穏やかさやリラックス感を促進させるものとして、心理的側面から採用された。この空間では直角は排除されている。デザインで次に重要だったのは照明と色彩であった。ニッチに組み込まれたり、間接照明の手法を用いることによりソフトな空間を演出している。色彩は全体に白でまとめ、奥の壁に鮮やかなオレンジ色を配し対比のコントラストをつけ子供達の元気さを引き出すようにしている。

曲線部分の多くはデジタルデータからCNC旋盤でカットされたMDFボードである。

（左上）レセプションブースのカウンター

(Left above) Counter in the reception booth

（右上）2階への階段

(Right above) Stairs to the 2nd floor

（右）2階の遊戯室
(Right) Play room on the 2nd floor

This is a newly opened section specializing in children with autism disorder within an existing medical center. The area is around 150 sq. m. wide. At the center is the reception counter which is integrated with a low wall. Around the reception area are three consulting rooms and one storeroom. The upper floor is a wide-open space for children to play together.

The voluminous partition walls and ceiling undulate, and curved louvers draw soft lines. These circulating lines and round lines are adopted as they give calm and relaxing feelings to people. In this space, right angles are excluded also from a psychological consideration. Lighting and colors are second important elements in designing this section. Lighting fixtures are installed in niches or behind furniture pieces to produce a soft atmosphere. White is the key color to which orange is used in the back as an accent to enliven children. Many of the curved walls and ceiling are made of medium-density fiberboards (MDF) cut by a computer numerical controlled (CNC) lathe.

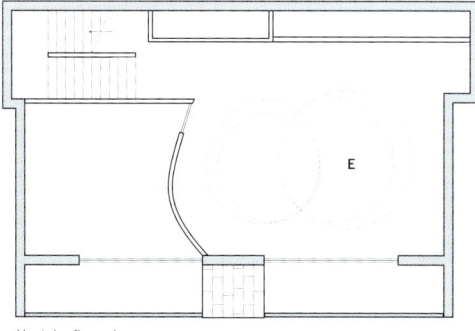

Upstairs floor plan

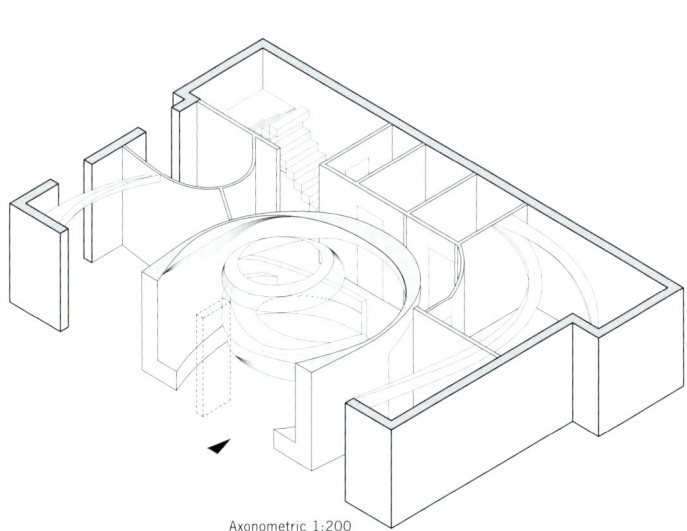

Axonometric 1:200

A: Receptionist
B: Medical consultation room
C: Storage
D: WC
E: Play room

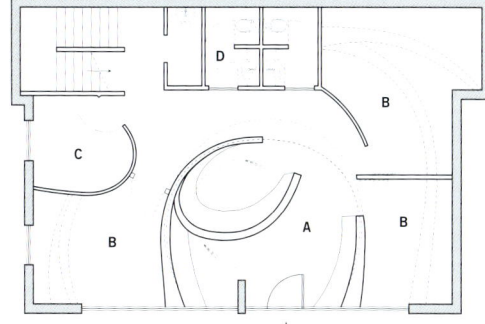

Ground floor plan 1:200

Paco Roncero's Workshop

Gastromic reserch workshop / Madrid

Designer: Carmen Baselga

Article: Yasuhiko Taguchi
Photography: Gerald Kiernan

五感と食の実験場

入り口側より見た全景
Whole interior viewed from the entrance side

照明で室内の雰囲気を変えることができる
Interior atmosphere is changeable by
manipulating lighting

a
b
c

このプロジェクトはミシュランにも紹介され、独創的スペイン料理で知られたパコ・ロンセロの新しい料理を開発するワークショップである。新しい料理の開発と平行して、感情と知覚面から食を実験するという目的も持ち、二つのアプローチで食の世界を掘り下げる場である。

料理と環境の間の関係を調査する項目は、例えば「ある種の色、形、味から人間がどのようにそれを知覚していくか」「温度、湿度、音、光等によって変わりやすい環境の快適さとは何か」「新しい感情のもとになる異なった感覚を作り出すには」「味覚の重要な要素である共感を共有するには」等をベースにコンセプトがつくられた。

空間デザインの目的は時代の特性を生かし、過去と現在の違いを重ね合わせることができる白い箱を作ることであった。スペースは非常に細長く幅より天井が高いという特別なプロポーションをもっている。両端に大きなドアがあり、一つはワークショップをサポートするオフィスにつながり、他のドアはカジノ・デ・マドリッド（1903年建造の社交クラブ）に続きゲストの出入口になっている。高い天井から吊り下げられたパネルはプロジェクターのスクリーン、異なった照明、音、香り等いろいろな機能を備え、可変性のあるスペースにデザイ

ンされた。壁面にはシェフの216種のオリーブオイル・コレクションが背後から照明され、部屋にアクセントを与えている。壁面の上部からは可動アームが伸び、スクリーンが付けられ異空間の演出とプレゼンテーションに使用されている。

このワークショップはプライベートな仕事の場で、一般には公開されていない。特別なランチや新しい試みのディナー等、リサーチ目的のためにシェフは特別の招待客だけを受け入れている。

（上上）オリーブオイル・コレクションの壁面ディスプレイ

(Above above) Wall display for the chef's collection of olive oil

（左上）シンク付きのエントランスホール

(Right) The entrance hall with a sink

（右上）壁面ディスプレイのディテール

(Above) Detail of the wall display

（上・右上）食と雰囲気に関する実験風景

(Above right Above) Experimenting scene on relations between gastronomy and the interior atmosphere

The space is the research workshop of Michelin chef Paco Roncero, known for his creative takes on Spanish cuisine, and this is where he develops new dishes. It is a place to experiment, in both of its meanings, ie. testing, but also experimenting with the meaning of "feeling and perceiving." The workshop will allow an exploration of the relationships between gastronomy and the environment. According to the designer, the concept includes "human perception from the influence of, for example, certain colors, shapes and flavors; or from …temperature, humidity, sound and light, manipulated in the search of well-being, or looking to generate different types of sensations that result in emotions…"
The aim of the design was to create a white box that kept the character of its time and allows the difference between the past and present to be seen in a superimposed way. The room has peculiar proportions; it is very long and is taller than it is wide. There is a big entrance door at each end, with one linking to an office to support workshop operation. The other connects to the Casino de Madrid (a social club built in 1903), and this is where guests will enter and leave. A central tray hanging from the high ceiling was designed to be flexible, housing different types of lighting, projectors, cameras, scent diffusers, extraction systems and other equipment. In the upper part of the tray, two mechanical arms move projection screens that are used to create differ-

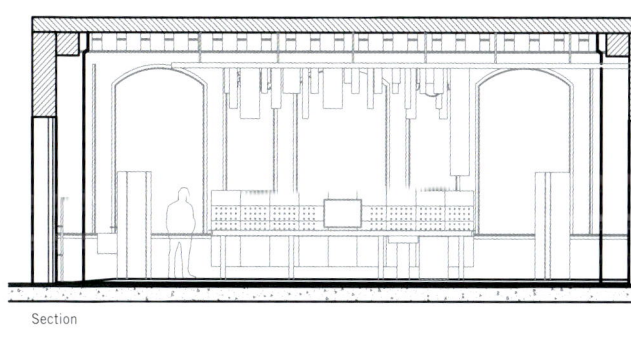

Section

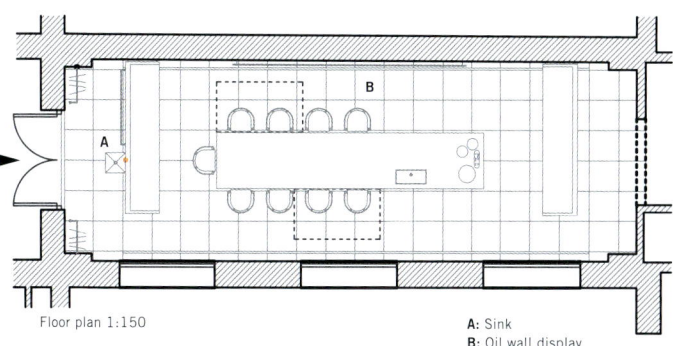

Floor plan 1:150

A: Sink
B: Oil wall display

ent atmospheres and/or for projecting images onto the table. Along the wall, there is a display for the chef's collection of 216 types of olive oil, which is lighted from behind and adds accent to the space.
As it is a private work area, it is not accessible to the general public. For the special lunches or experimental dinners, the chef extends invitations for research purposes.

Designer: Carmen Baselga_Taller de Proyectos in collaboration with S3-Tau
Total area: 46.45 m² + Office 24.5 m²
Client: Paco Roncero
Completion: Jul. 2012
Main materials: Ceramic, wood
Site: "Casino de Madrid", in C/Alcalá number 15, Madrid

アルステルダムのスキポール国際空港内にAKOの
フラッグシップ店がオープンした。インテリアは全
て本をテーマにデザインされ、本の形をした展示台、
本の照明器具、本を積み重ねたキャッシャーカウ
ンター等がシンプルなフロアプランの中で形作ら
れた。
店頭は通路に対して広く開かれ、黒い天井を背景
に、宙を飛ぶ本のカーペットのような照明器具は
スペースに躍動感を与えている。本のカラフルな
装丁が引き立つように、店内は白と黒をベースに
デザインされている。大きなブックリボンは天井や
床に伸び、赤とブルーでアクセントが付けられ、店
内の本を探すナビゲーションの役割を果たしている。
場所柄ここでは主に旅行関係の本が扱われてい
る。またショップ・イン・ショップとして、旅行も
のを扱う出版社Loney planetとNational geo
graphic社のコーナーが作られている。これから
訪問する土地の情報を得たい人、あるいはエキゾ
チックな観光地へ夢を馳せる人々のために本がゆっ
くり読める場所も設けている。

Opening within Amsterdam's Schiphol Airport is AKO's flagship bookstore. Based on a simple floor plan, the interior is
completely designed with the theme of books in mind, with
book-shaped display shelves, book-shaped lighting fixtures,
and a cashier's counter that is a stack of books.
The shop opens wide to the corridor, and with the black
ceiling as the background, a flock of books take flight,
serving as the lighting fixtures and adding movement to the
space. The black and white shop interior makes the colorful
book covers stand out. Large bookmarks stretch from the
floor to the ceiling with red and blue accents and function
as book-finding navigation in the store.
Due to its location, the shop handles mainly travel-related
publications. Also located within the space are Lonely Planet
and National Geographic corners as shop-in-shops. There is
a reading area for travelers who can look up their destination
or for armchair travelers to dream about foreign locales.

AKO Books
& Travel

Designer: Tjep

Article: Yasuhiko Taguchi
Photography: Tjep; Yannic
Alidarso and Martynika

Book store / Amsterdam

本の
ワンダーランド

Inspire people to care about the plane

NATIONAL
GEOGRAPHIC

（上）本の売り場検索コーナー

(Above) Book-finding navigation corner

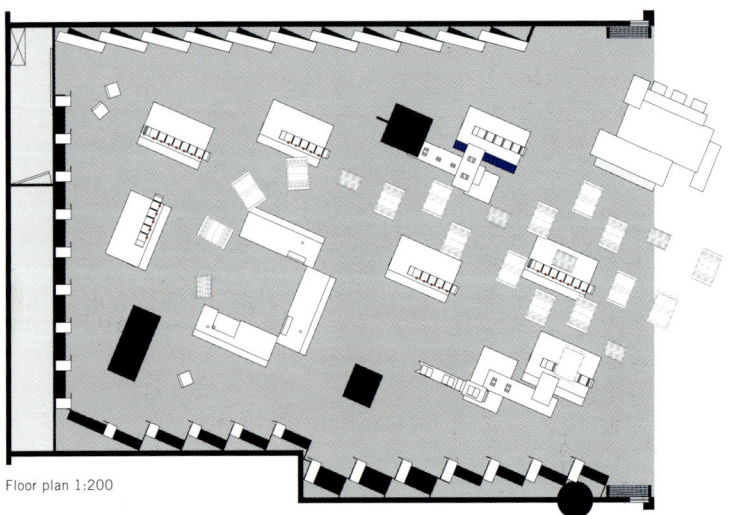

Floor plan 1:200

Design firm: Tjep
Designer: Frank Tjepkema, Leonie Janssen
Total area: 200 m²
Contractor: Hemi
Completion: Jun. 2012
Site: Schiphol Airport, Amsterdam

（上）本の平台も本の形

(Above) Display table for books also in the shape of a book

（左下）家具の脚部ディテール

(Left bottom) Detail of the leg of furniture

（右下）入り口左手のディスプレイを見る

(Right above) View of the display on the left side from the entrance

Fudge Pop-up
Hair Salon

Pop-up hair salon / London

Designer:
Zaha Hadid Architects

Article: Yasuhiko Taguchi
Photography:
Marcus Peel, Courtesy of
Zaha Hadid Architects

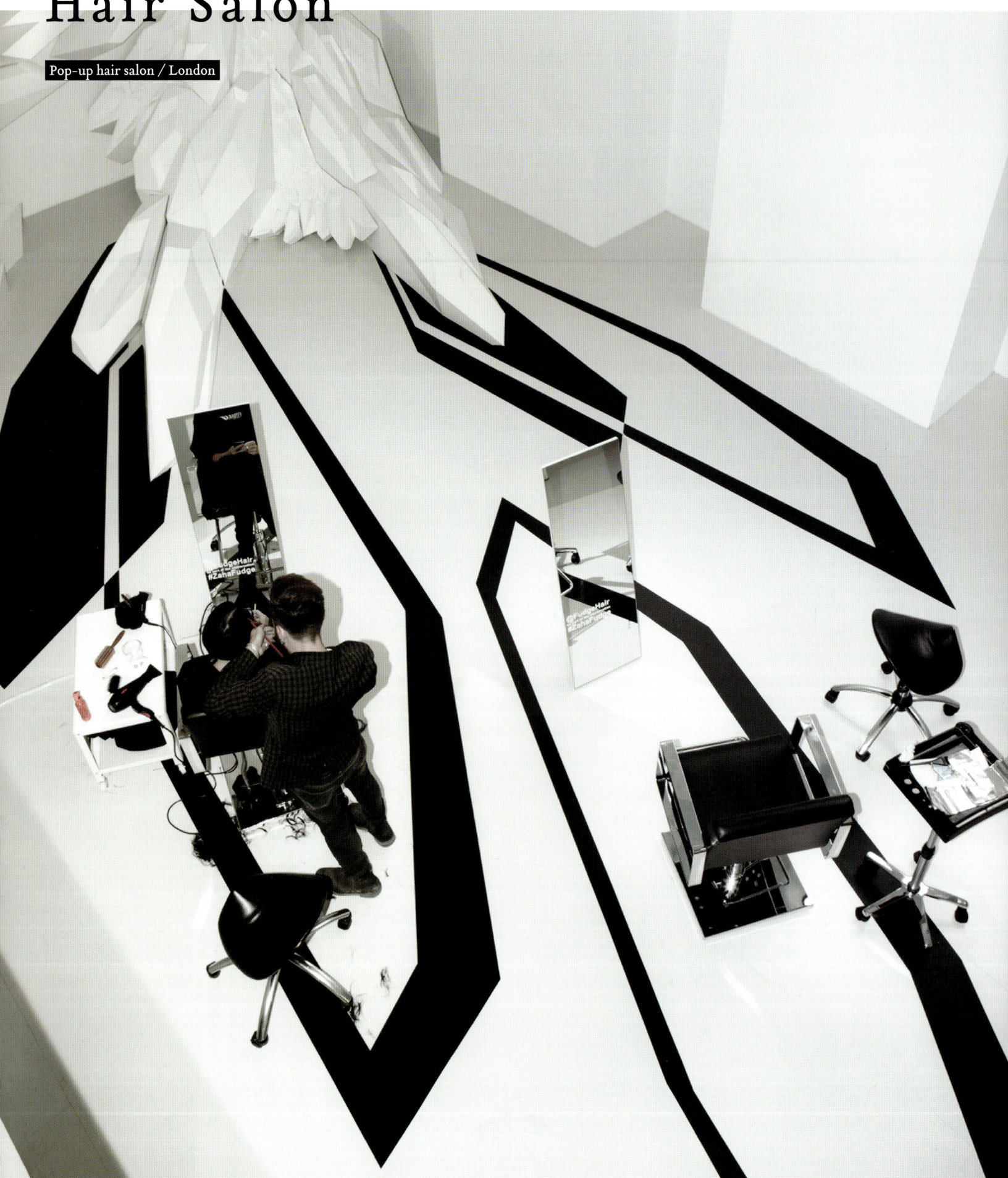

（左）レンダリング
(Left) Rendering

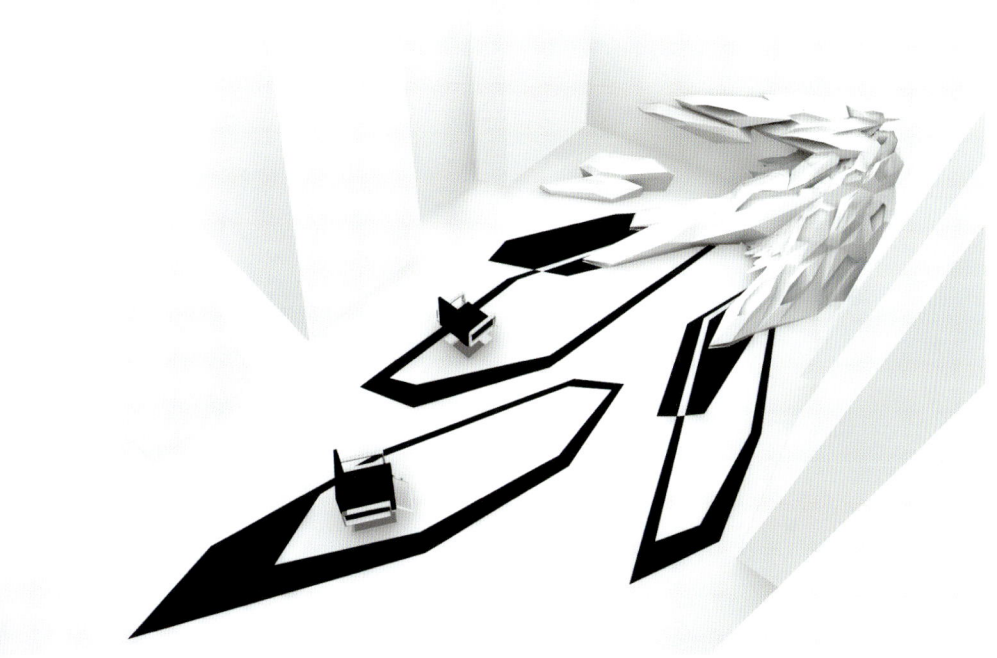

髪の
オブジェがある
ヘアサロン

（左頁・右）ポップアップサロン（期間限
定サロン）俯瞰

(Left page, right) Overlooking the Pop
up salon

Design firm: Zaha Hadid Architects
Concept: Zaha Hadid, John Vial (Fudge);
Design: Zaha Hadid, Patrik Schumacher
Project team: Karine Yassine, Filipa Gomes, Maha Kutay, Henry Virgin, Claudia Fruianu, Mirren Rosie
Gallery team: Shaun Farrell, Soomeen Hahn, Maren Klasing, Thomas Soo, Maria Araya, Kevin Sheppard
Client: Fudge Hair
Period: Sep. 21–Oct. 13, 2012
Main materials: Laminated polyurethane resin, Acrylic, Wallpaper, Cardboard
Site: Zaha Hadid Design Gallery, London

（左）Fudge ヘアーのイメージ

(Left) Fudge hair image

（上）しなやかな髪をイメージしたアートワーク

(Above) Art works in the image of silky-smooth hair

For the cult hair salon brand Fudge, Zaha Hadid Design Gallery produced its first pop-up salon, which was open for London Fashion Week and London Design Week.
Fudge was recently purchased by the cosmetics company PZ Cussons Beauty, and this salon was planned as an event to help boost consumer awareness. The Fudge Pop-Up Salon will not only present its leading creative geniuses for hair advice and styling, cutting, and color, but the collaboration will also showcase unique designs from the Zaha Hadid Architects.
Zaha Hadid has a deep connection with art, fashion and architecture and she comments about these three elements: "there exists much more fluidity now... more cross pollination in the disciplines which can be built upon in collaborations and exploring what these practices and processes can contribute to one another."
"The future of Fudge is about developing relationships with like-minded challenging brands, pushing forward our individuality, and really standing out from others," notes Fudge Creative Director John Vial.
The Zaha Hadid Design Gallery melds these three different elements, while works that represent the softness and silky-smoothness of hair are displayed within the white space like works of art.
This pop-up salon became a new and active starting point for impressing upon consumers the brand's direction.

ザハ・ハディドはカルト的雰囲気をもつヘアサロンブランド、ファッジのためにロンドンのファッションウィークとデザインウィークに合わせてブランド初のポップアップサロンをデザインした。
ファッジは最近化粧品メーカーPZクソンズのビューティー部門が買収し、消費者の認知度を高めるイベントのひとつとしてこのサロンは企画された。この分野のクリエイティブなリーダーとしてヘアのアドバイス、スタイリング、ヘアカッティングやヘアカラーだけでなく、ザハ・ハディドと協力することによってサロンをユニークなデザインのショーケースにすることを目指した。
「ザハ・ハディドの作品はアート、ファッション、建築と深く結びつき、この3分野の中において非常に

流動的に存在し、各分野が相互に混じり、お互いの良さが引き出されている。ファッジの将来はブランドの挑戦と不可分であり、個性を押し伸ばし差別化を作り出し、同じ心をもった人々との関係を強めることである」とファッジのクリエーティブ・ディレクターのジョン・バイアル氏は述べている。
ザハ・ハディド・デザインギャラリーには三つの異なった分野が融合されるようなザハ・ハディドの、髪の毛の柔らかさや、しなやかな髪のイメージが伝わる作品が白い空間にアートのように展示された。このポップアップサロンはより幅広い消費者向けにブランドの方向性を示す新しい活動の出発点となった。

セットブース

Hairdo booth

Chatachol
Hair Salon

Hair salon / Bangkok

Designer: NKDW

Article: Yasuhiko Taguchi
Photography:
Nattapon Klinsuwan

レセプションエリアよりスタイリングエリア
を見る

Styling area viewed from the reception area

バンコックの中心地にあるターミナル21ショッピングセンター内に、この街のグリーンシティ・イメージを反映するヘアサロンがオープンした。コンセプトは、竹が天井からいろいろの長さに吊り下がってインテリア空間を包むというもの。

デザイナーは、タイ南部を旅行した時に訪れた自然の洞窟からこのアイデアのヒントを得た。洞窟では鍾乳石と石筍がつながり柱になったり、壁面を形成したりして自然のスペース内に部屋が作られている。

店は、人が洞窟に入ったときそうするように、あちこち興味をもちながら店内を移動できるよう、各エリアを壁やパーティションで仕切るかわりに竹による彫刻的空間が作られた。壁と天井の間のラインが自然と融け込むように、天井から異なったサイズの竹竿が吊り下げられているが、一部を床近くまで届くように吊り下げ、各エリアを分割した。この方法でカラーリングとシャンプーエリアのスクリーンも作られた。

デザイナーは予算をコントロールできて、エコロジカルな場所を作れる、一石二鳥の方法として地元の材料を使用することにし、木材の代わりに成長の速い竹を使用した。タイの東部から11,250本の異なったサイズの竹が集められ、プロジェクトはその地域の人々に経済的メリットも与えた。

竹 の 洞 窟

Opening in the Terminal 21 shopping complex in the heart of Bangkok, a hair salon explores the metropolis' image as a Green City. The concept includes an interior space that appears to be wrapped by numerous bamboo sticks hanging from the ceiling in different levels.

The designer was inspired by the natural space of caves while he was traveling in the southern Thailand. In caves, rock formations called stalactites and stalagmites sometimes connect, forming walls and creating rooms within the cavern.

The shop interior is a sculpture that people can walk through and explore, like a cave, and instead of walls or partitions to separate working areas, the shop interior is divided by bamboo. Different lengths of bamboo sticks hang down from the ceiling, and some poles are long enough to reach the floor, blurring the line between wall and ceiling. This also creates walls that screen off the coloring and shampooing areas.

The designer chose to employ local materials in order to control costs and to create an eco-friendly place, and as such, focused on bamboo, a fast-growing material and alternative to timber. The project collected 11,250 bamboo poles of different sizes from Eastern Thailand, and this approach brought economic benefits to the local population.

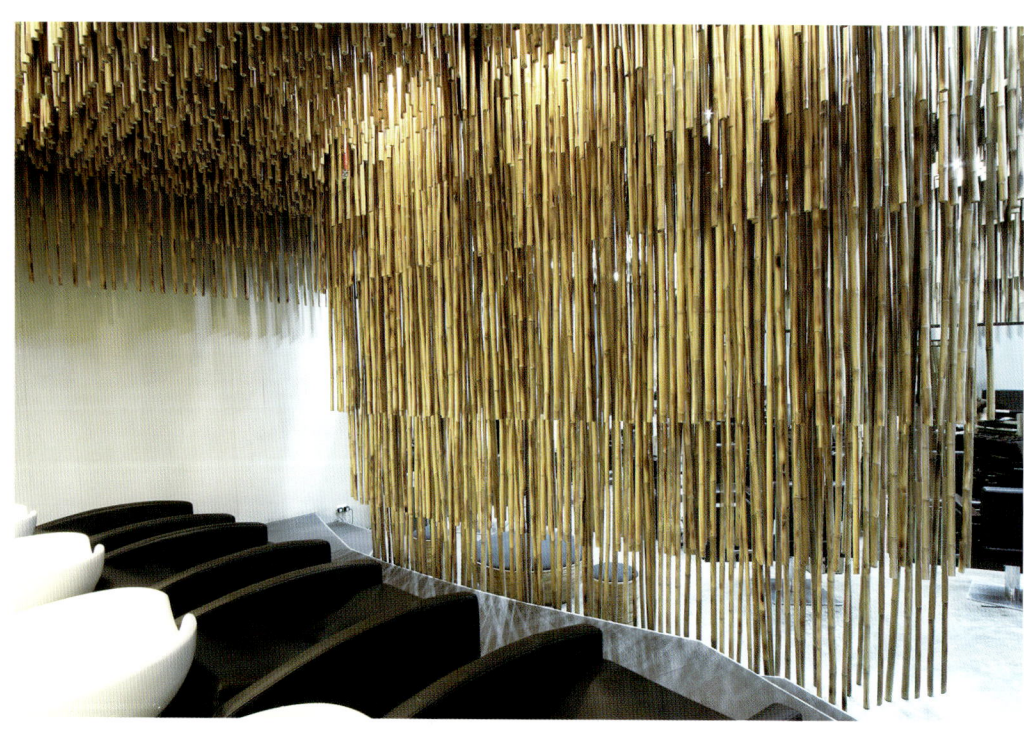

（上）スタイリングエリアの奥部。左手に
シャンプーエリア

（下）シャンプーエリアから竹のパーティ
ションを見る

(Above) The inner part of the styring
area. The shampoo area on the left

(Bottom) Bamboo partitions viewed
from the shampoo area

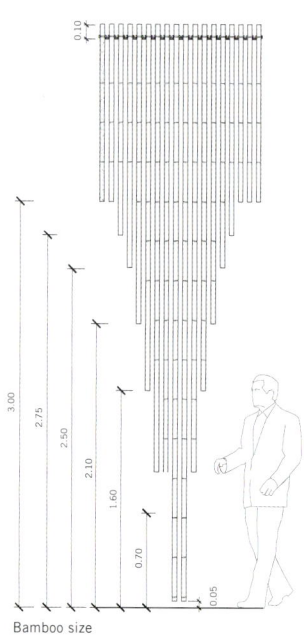

Bamboo size

Design firm: NKDW
Designer: Nattapon Klinsuwan
Total area: 107 m²
Contractor: A-Ron
Client: Chalachol
Completion: Nov. 2011
Construction cost: $120,000
Main materials: Bamboo sticks, Polished concrete floor, Artificial wood panelling; Shera
Site: Shopping Mall; 2,88 Sukhumvit Soi 19Sukhumvit Rd. North Klongtoei, Wattana, Bangkok

SPA-DE Vol.19

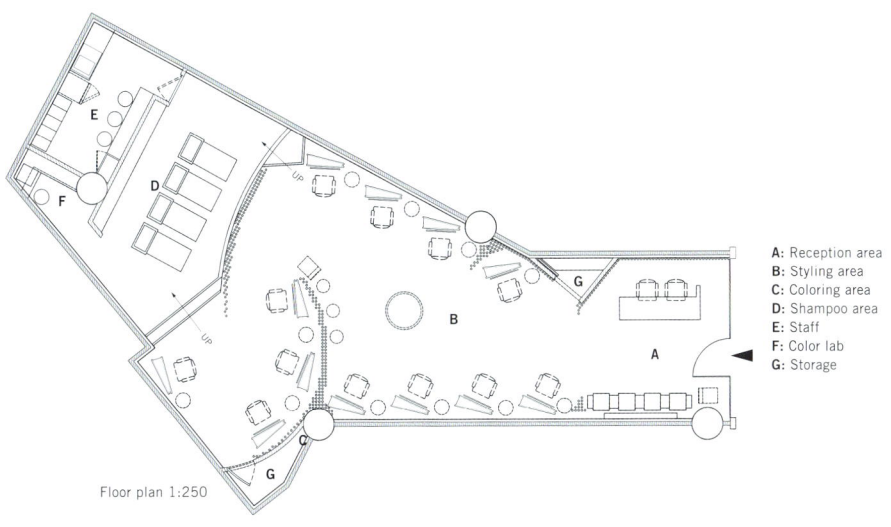

Floor plan 1:250

A: Reception area
B: Styling area
C: Coloring area
D: Shampoo area
E: Staff
F: Color lab
G: Storage

（上）円形の竹の装飾を見上げる

(Above) Looking up at the round pattern bamboo ornament

鍾乳洞に
挿入された
氷山

（左頁）入り口より店内を見る

(Left page) Looking into the bar from the entrance

（上）入り口まわり外観

(Above) View of the entrance

（右）LED照明により空間の雰囲気は自由に変えられる

(Right) The chromatic tones can be freely changed by LED lighting

É Prá Poncha

Nightclub and Bar / Porto, Portugal

Designer: António Fernandez Architects

Article: Ikunori Ara
Photography: José Campos

É Prá Ponchaは、ポルトガル、ポート市の夜の繁華街にあるナイトクラブ＆バーである。

奥行きがあって狭い、デザインしづらい店をデザイナーは、氷や鍾乳石が融解して滴が落ちて来る形をイメージして設計した。あたかも自然の洞窟内の天井を模したかのように、カーブしたラッカー塗装のMDFが天井一面に並べられた。これらの折り重なるフィンは、有機的かつ機能的に顧客のエリアとスタッフのエリアを分けている。既存の御影石の壁面は、さらに洞窟らしくするためグレーで塗装され。一部の深い溝はPVCのミラー貼りになっていて、その照明の反射は歪みと温かさを醸し出している。そして天井にはLEDの照明が組み込まれていて、いろいろな調節が可能である。色のグラデーションも容易で、夜には徐々に店内の雰囲気を変化させることができる。バーカウンターは半透明のコーリアン（人造大理石）で出来ていて、白色が氷の反射のようであり、氷山が水に浮いているかのようにも見える。

É Prá Poncha is a nightclub and bar situated in the nightlife area of Porto, Portugal. With a difficult deep but narrow space the designer took inspiration from natural forms, water dripping from melting ice or stalactites hanging from a ceiling. Imitating these natural formations in a cave the entire ceiling is covered with lacquered MDF strata. These strata work both aesthetically and functionally, undulating to shape various spaces and chambers within the cave like space to give different experiences within the bar and staff working areas. The pre-existing granite walls are painted grey continuing the analogy to a cave. In the deeper chamber there are also mirrored surfaces, which along with the lighting create a feeling of distortion and warmth. The chromatic tones of the ceiling can be altered through a series of LED lights, which slowly change over the course of an evening. The bar counters, made from translucent Corian, reflect white light simulating ice, appearing like ice bergs floating in water.

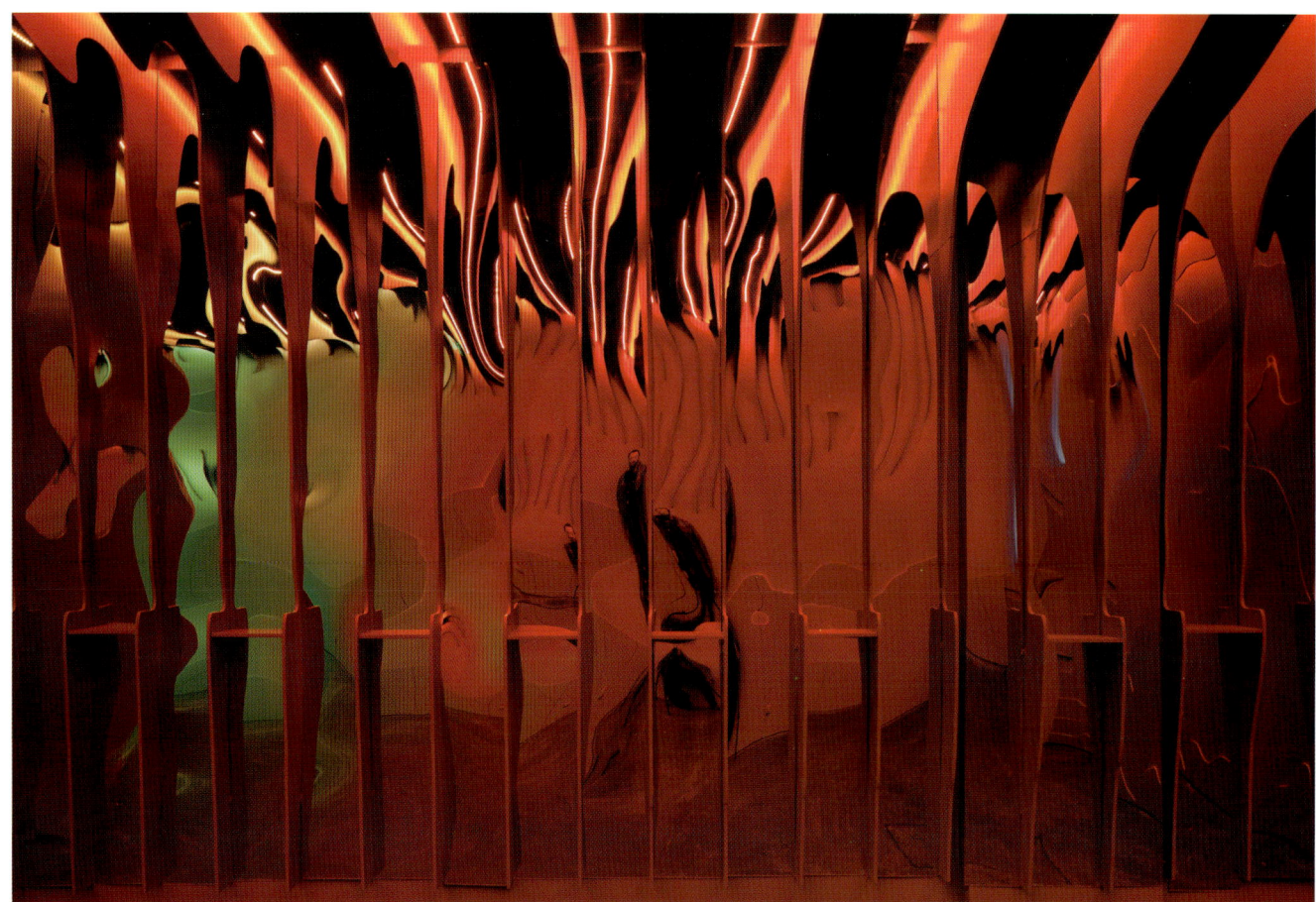

（上・左）店内右手奥のスタンディング席。
壁はミラー貼り

(Above, left) Standing area on the inner right side of the bar. The walls have mirrored surfaces

（右頁）奥より入り口方向見返し

(Right page) Looking back at the entrance from the inner part of the bar

Designer: António Fernandez Architects
Design team: António Fernandez, Ema Rosmaninho,
Client : Duarte, Elmano &Manuel Lda.
Total area: 140 m²
Completion: Apr. 2012
Main materials:
Ceiling & Wall- Sheets of lacquered MDF, Floor- Stroked screed concrete finish, Wall- Existing granite painted grey, Bar counter- Translucent Corian,
Lighting: LED lighting
Site: Rua da Galeria de Paris n° 99, R/ Ch, Porto, Portugal

A: Kitchen
B: Counter
C: Standing seats
D: WC
E: Office

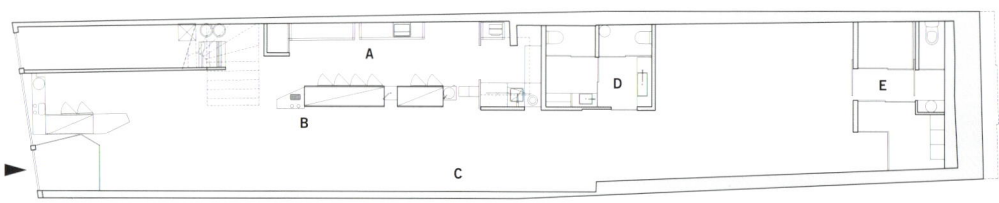

Floor plan

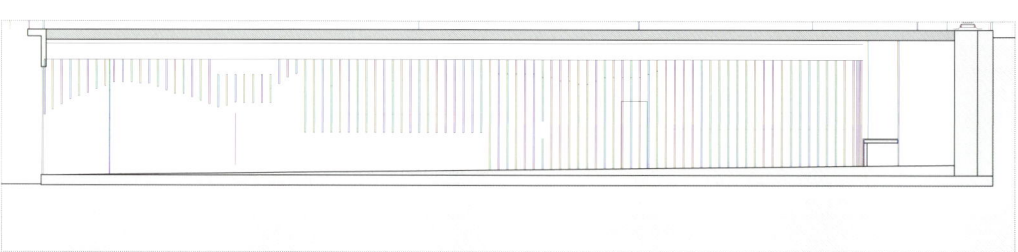

Section

Section

Eleven Inch
Pizzeria

Designer: Article: Ikunori Ara
Zwei Interiors Architecture   Photography: Michael Kai

（上）入り口側よりオープンキッチンを見る

(Above) Open kitchen viewed from the
entrance side

（右）入り口側より大テーブル席を見る

(Right) Communal table seats viewed
from the entrance side

ウオールサイズド・
グラフィック

（上）オープンキッチン側より大テーブル
席を見る

(Above) Communal table seats viewed
from the open kitchen side

（上）トイレ側のカウンター席
(Above) Counter seats by the lavatory

A: Counter table **E:** Kitchen
B: Communal table **F:** M.WC
C: Dish-up **G:** Unisex WC
D: Show case

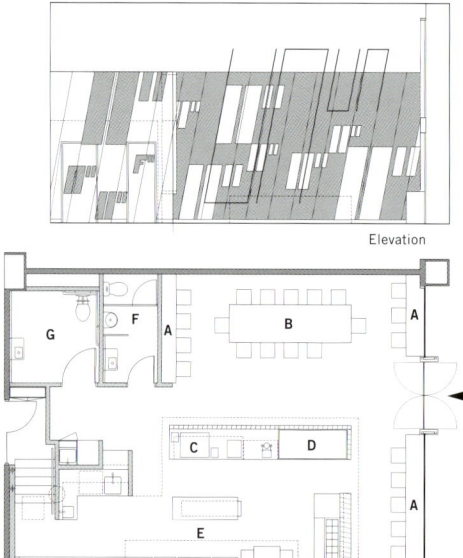

Elevation

Floor plan 1:200

メルボルンのドックランドに位置する「イレブンインチ・ピッツェリア」は伝統的なピザのテイクアウトショップであるがそのデザインはユニークである。シンプルな色とグラフィックは、遊び心があって強い印象を与えている。特に目立つのは黒色の壁面をバックにグラフィカルに傾いだ合板を取付けたダブルスキンの壁。それと同じ合板のコミューナルテーブルである。そしてテーブルの上のアクセントとキッチン天井のライムグリーンが、グラフィカルな壁面に対比されたこの空間のもう一つのフォーカルポイントになっている。

キッチン上部の下がり壁には明るいグリーンのアルミニウムのフィンが取付けられ、シャープな印象を店内にもたらしている。表し天井には極少数のLED照明があるだけで、昼は店舗前面よりの自然光、そして夜はテーブル上の高さの異なる黒のペンダントで照度を得ている。スツールは、Emiliana Design studioがデザインした"Naoshima stool"で、木のフレームに折り曲げたベニヤ板の黒い座が、連続したオブジェのようである。

Architects: Zwei Interiors Architecture
Design team: Hanna Richardson, Katherine Kemp & Alberto Vallesi
Client: Eleven Inch
Total area: 93 m²
Completion: Jan. 2012
Contractor: FSCI
Main Materials: Plywood, Anodised aluminium
Site: Shop 8 Village street, 737 bourke street, Docklands, Melbourne

Situated in Docklands, Melbourne, the Eleven Inch Pizzeria is a traditional pizzeria take-away with a surprising interior. The simple colours and graphic forms create a playful, bold impact. Surfaces are dominated by plywood in the wall cladding over the black walls and furniture with touches of lime on the tabletops and on the kitchen ceiling providing an alternative focal point to the graphic feature wall. The bulkhead is lined with angled luminous green aluminium fins creating an angular perspective within the space. The stripped back design exposes the ceiling with minimal LED lighting. Natural light is maximised through the shop front and there is staggered black Nord pendant lighting clustered over the communal tables. The restaurant uses the Naoshima stool designed by Emiliana Design studio. Made of timber, redefined as it is folded and curved and the stools appear as a continuous object.

SPA-DE Vol.19

Nanushka
Beta Store

Boutique / Budapest

Designer: Daniel Balo, Zsofi
Dobos, Dora Medveczky,
Judit Emese Konopas,
Noemi Varga

Article: Yasuhiko Taguchi
Photography:
Tamas Bujnovszky

キャンバスの
内側の世界

入り口側より店内を見る

View from the entrance side

キャッシュ＆ラップカウンターまわり
View arround the cash & wrap counter

ハンガリーの若手ファッションデザイナー、サンドラサンダーの秋冬コレクションのポップアップストアがブタペストのファッションストリートにオープンした。建築科の学生に依頼し、低予算、3週間という短期間で店がデザインされた。デザイン上の大きな制約はスペースが予想外に細長いのと、インテリアを疵つけず最低限のドリル穴だけでデザインすることであった。

デザイナーは彼女のブランドを反映する自然で温かいインテリアを求めた。デザインのインスピレーションとしてクラシックなウエディング・テントと納屋での結婚式から原野のイメージが採用され、木綿、麻、焚き木、錆びた鉄等がデザインの要素として集められた。

最初に天井の下にワイヤーを張り、250㎡のキャンバスでインテリアを包み込むシステムが考えられた。入口側から奥まで、キャンバスをワイヤーで吊り下げ、自然に垂れるようにして売り場スペースを内側から造り上げる方法である。

焚き木は輪切りになって床に貼られ、木は束ねられ床から突き出てきたようにテーブルとして使われた。スペースのオーガニックな雰囲気を出すために、同じシリンダー形の麻のブーツとバルーンの形をした照明がデザインされた。これに対し完全な幾何学的フォルムのカウンターと更衣室が作られ、錆びたスチールラックで布とのバランスがとられた。素朴で滑らかで柔らかな材料を使用することでブランドのサスティナブルなコンセプトが生かされた。

（左）既存天井からワイヤーで吊り下げられたキャンバス

(Left) Canvas suspended with wire from the ceiling

（上）店内最奥部

(Above) Innermost part of the store

Opening on Budapest's fashion street was a pop-up store for young Hungarian fashion designer Sandra Sandor's fall/winter collection. A handpicked team of design school graduates created the store with a limited budget and in three short weeks. The project required a design that would leave the interior unharmed, with only minor drilling permitted, and that would accommodate a retail space with an unusually elongated shape.

The fashion designer aimed for a natural, warm interior that would reflect her brand. As inspiration for the design, the team chose the theme of wilderness and elements from traditional wedding tents and barn weddings. As such, they gathered together raw materials such as cotton, linen, firewood, and rusted steel for the design.

First they created a rigging system for the 250 square-meter canvas that would drape the interior by pulling wires below the ceiling. From the front to the back, they hung the canvas and let it fall and flow in a way that wrapped the entire retail space from the inside.

The team created the flooring by slicing firewood into circles and laying them out, and small display stands made from logs seem to sprout from the ground. In order to strengthen the organic flow of the space, linen poufs and balloon lamps sharing the same cylindrical shape were used. Meanwhile, the strictly geometric forms of the counter and fitting rooms, as well as the rusted steel racks, created balance to the space. The use of these simple, smooth, and soft materials helped enhance the design's concept of sustainability.

Designer: Daniel Balo, Zsofi Dobos, Dora Medveczky, Judit Emese Konopas, Noemi Varga
Consultant: Lamps-Ballon Lamp Hungary
Total area: 80 m²
Contractor: Tamas Lindwurm- Honti Kft.
Client: Sandra Sandor- Nanushka
Opening period: Nov. 2011–Feb. 2012
Design and construction period: 3 weeks
Budget: 2,000 Euro
Main materials: Canvas, firewood
Site: Fashion Street, Budapest

Shoebaloo Maastricht

Shoe shop / Maastricht

SPA-DE Vol.19

Designer:
Meyer en Van Schooten
Architecten (MVSA)

Article: Masaatsu Fukazawa
Photography:
Jeroen Musch

彫り込まれた等高線

Design firm: Meyer en Van Schooten Architecten (MVSA)
Project manager: Harry van den Berg
Consultant: Installation consultancy- HVL BV, 's-Hertogenbosch
Lighting- Ansorg , Ouderkerk a/d Amstel, Zumtobel, Breda
Flooring- DRT Vloeren, Oss
Total area: 46 m²
Contractor: Smeulders Interieurgroep, Nuenen
Client: Shoebaloo BV, Amsterdam
Completion: Mar. 2012
Main materials: Floor- finished with a print motif and a transparent PU topcoat
Wall- MDF, polished aluminium,
Shelves- MDF, polished aluminium, royal blue artificial suede
Site: Stokstraat 25A, Maastricht

（左上）ファサード

(Left above) Facade

（左下）店内奥エリア

(Left bottom) Inner part in the store

（下）ディスプレイ棚のディテール

(Bottom) Detail of the display shelves

オランダの高級デザイナー・シューズ、バッグで有名なShoebalooは国内主要都市にショップを展開している。このマーストリヒト店は6番目のショップである。

インテリアデザインは建築界で活躍するアムステルダムの設計集団MVSAで、アムステルダム P.C. Hooftstrrat 店も彼らのデザインである。

店はマーストリヒトの中心部で文化遺産の多い地域にあり、建物保存のためファサードは変えることができなかった。そのためウインドー部に、枠は変えずに楕円の窓を取り付けたデザインになっている。

しかし中に入ると面積46㎡の小さい店は、金属の洞窟のような、宇宙船の中に入ったような異空間だ。プランは楕円を二つ組み合わせたような有機形で、壁は、鏡面仕上げの無数のアルミバンドで等高線のように構成されている。まるで渓谷の侵食された地層のように手前に突き出たり窪んだり、アルミ鏡面の小口の棚が切れ目なく続きダイナミックな景観を作り出している。

このアルミの等高線は徹底して使用され、キャッシュカウンターや、ハンドバックやアクセサリー展示のためのニッチのキャビネット、さらに試着用スツールまでもが等高線エレメントで作られている。

棚面はロイヤルブルー色の人工スエード貼り。床はプリントされたシルエットのデザインで透明ポリウレタンの上塗り仕上げである。

Shoebaloo is a famous high-end designer shoe and handbag retailer in the Netherlands. This store in Maastricht is its sixth outlet.

MVSA, a renowned Amsterdam-based architectural firm designed the interior of the store following the store in P.C. Hoofstrrat in Amsterdam.

The store is in the heart of Maastricht with many historical buildings. The facade could not be changed because of the restrictions to preserve the building. Therefore, oval windows are installed to the existing window frames.

Upon entering the store, you may feel like you are put into a different dimension. The interior of the 46 sq. m wide store is like a metallic cave or a space ship. It has an organic floor space combining two ellipsoids. The walls are composed of numerous mirror-finished aluminum bands arranged like contour lines. Shelves are made like eroded layers in a canyon, some are recessed and others jut out. The alternating layers of shiny edges and matt-leather surfaces of shelves create a dynamic and exciting landscape.

The contour lines are applied to all interior elements, such as a cashier counter, niche cabinets for displaying handbags and accessories, and even to stools for customers to try shoes. The shelf boards are finished in artificial suede. The floor is finished with a printed flooring material on which transparent polyurethane topcoat is applied.

（下）入り口方向見返し
(Bottom) Loking back at the entrance from the inner part

Section

Floor plan

A: SW
B: Casher counter

Camper 20 years in Paris

Pop up store / Paris

Designer:
Studio François Dumas

Article: Ikunori Ara
Photography:
François Dumas

棒 の 魔 術

（上）1階奥より入り口方向見返し

(Above) Looking back at the entrance
from the 1st floor inner part

（右）外観夜景

(Right) Exterior view at night

（上）ディスプレイステージを奥から見る

(Above) Display stage viewed from the 1st floor inner part

（左下）オープニングレセプション風景

(Left bottom) Sciene from the opening reception

（下）ディスプレイシステム詳細

(Bottom) Detail of the display system

（上）2階の壁面展示　　　　　　　　　　　（左）2階の壁面展示のディテール
(Above) Wall display on the 2nd floor　　　(Left) Detail of the wall display on the 2nd floor

アムステルダム在住のフラン人デザイナーFrancois Dumasは、スペインの靴ブランド、カンペール20周年記念イベントのために、パリ・ファッションウイーク期間中だけの仮設店舗をデザインした。
このインスタレーションは主に塗装仕上げの「棒」により構築したもので、ローコストながら容易に設置、撤去もできるうえ、靴をディスプレイするにはこの上なくカラフルでダイナミックな方法である。「棒」は大量生産した後、ペイント槽の中に入れ塗装したり、切ったり、接続したりして形状を変えて使用している。店舗の1階では自立した構造棚や靴ごとのディスプレイスタンド、それに壁面アートワークを作製した。
2階以上はパーティー用のスペースである。カラフルな「棒」による壁面ディスプレイで靴を一つづつ展示した2階があり、3階では照明と一体化したオブジェが床置きされたり天井から下がったりしている。この仮店舗は遊び心いっぱいのデザインであるとともに、カンペールのブランド哲学をはっきり示したと言えるだろう。

Francois Dumas, a French designer based in Amsterdam, created a temporary shop installation for the Spanish shoe brand Camper to honour their 20th anniversary during Paris Fashion week.

This installation, mainly constructed of painted sticks, was an inexpensive, easy to install and dismantle, colourful and dynamic way of displaying shoes.

The sticks, industrially produced in large numbers, were customised by dipping in paint, cut and stapled together.

On the ground floor there was a free standing wooden shelving unit with display stick platforms to highlight the shoes and also an art work made from the sticks on the wall.

The two floors above were party spaces, rays of coloured sticks framed individual shoes on the first floor and on the second floor sticks formed lighting installations and footwear was hung from the ceiling. This pop up shop was extremely playful and imaginative illustrating the Camper brand's philosophy.

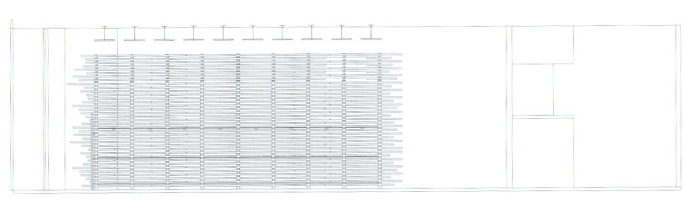

Section

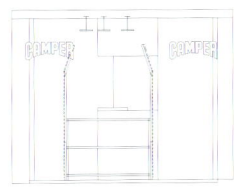

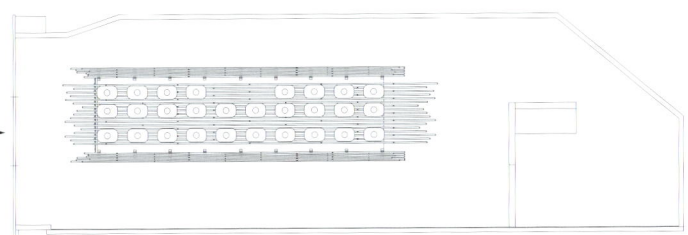

Floor plan

Designer: Studio François Dumas
Total area: 120 m² (3 floor 40 m² each)
Client: Camper Together
Completion: Sep. 2012
Main materials: Painted wood sticks
Site: Rue du Faubourg St. Honoré, Paris

（左上・右上）3階の床と天井のディスプレイ

(Left above, right above) Floor and ceiling displays on the 3rd floor

（左）ファサード
(Left) Facade

（下）店内奥より入り口方向見返し
(Bottom) Loking back at the entrance from the inner side

（右頁）店内左側を見る
(Right page) View of the store left side

Camper Steps

Shoe shop / Lyon

Designer:
Studio Makkink & Bey

Article: Ikunori Ara
Photography:
Sanchez y Montoro

靴のブランドCamperは、オランダのデザイン事務所Studio Makkink & Beyにフランス、リヨンの新店デザインを依頼した。「部屋の中の部屋」というアイデアのもとに、グラフィックを印刷した伸縮するファブリックのパネルを作製し、それを既存店舗の壁面に触らずに設置することにした。これらのパネルは容易に取り外せ、他のショップに移設することも可能である。
階段はその機能上靴の展示に適しているだけでなく、座ったり、話したり、通過したり、靴を試しに履いたりするには良い場所であるということから、歩くという人の基本的動作や階段での動きからインスパイアされたデザインとなった。

靴のディスプレイ用に赤い縁取りがついたチップボードでできた実物の階段も作製した。また、踏み台としての小さめの階段もいくつか作製し、腰掛けたり、靴の試着にも使用できるようにした。これらと連携して白い壁に描いた赤い線の階段や床のグラフィックは、奥行きを感じる錯覚を与えて、店舗を広く感じさせている。また店内を煩雑にすることのないよう、使用色は白、赤、黒のシンプルな色に留めて商品が目立つように配慮している。床は白のアクリル塗装。ディスプレイ用の埋め込み式の棚は黒と白。それに棒状ハロゲン照明を合わせている。

The shoe brand Camper commissioned Dutch design Studio Makkink & Bey to create a design for their new store in Lyon, France. The idea of creating "a room within a room" was realised with walls made of panels of stretch fabric printed with graphics, which do not actually touch the existing walls of the shop. These panels can be easily removed and can be installed in any shop.
The designers were inspired by the basic movement of walking and stairs as a perfect place for shoes or a place to sit, talk, pass through or try shoes on. There is a real staircase made of chipboard panelled with laminate outlined in red used for product display, several smaller sets used as step ladders and to sit and try footwear on and also stairs drawn in red on the white walls. The graphics on the walls and floor also show lines of basic walking movement giving an illusion of depth, making the small space appear much larger. Keeping the store clutter free with a minimal colour scheme of just white, red and black also helps and does not detract from the product. The flooring is white acrylic, with black and white recessed shelving units for display and halogen strip lights.

空間で機能する
階段のステッチ

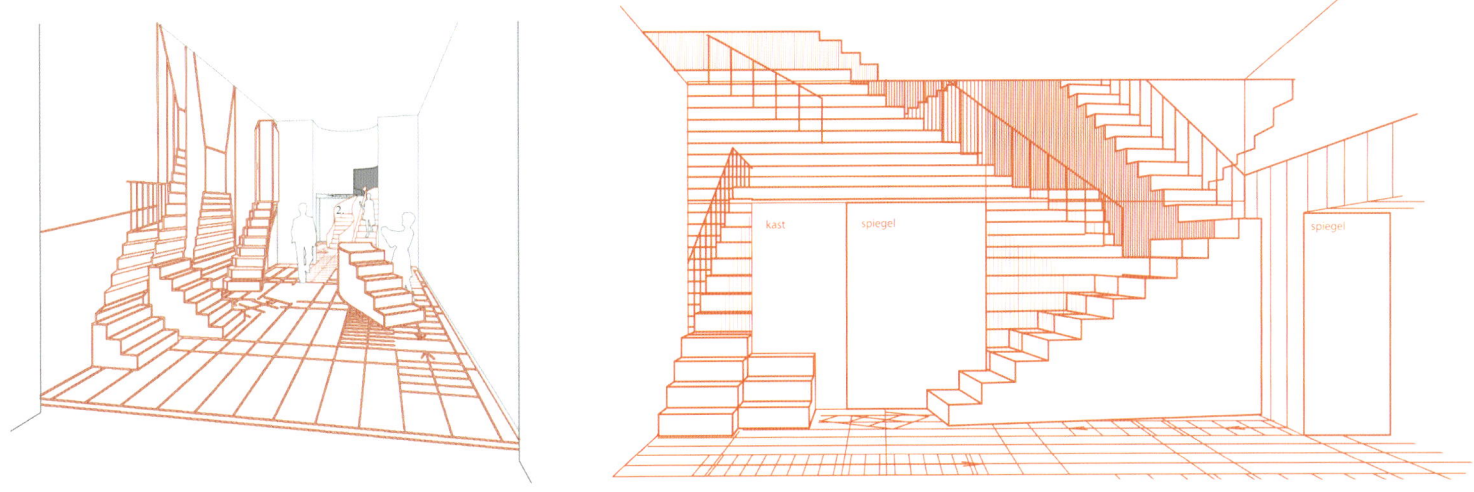

kast   spiegel   spiegel

Designer: Studio Makkink & Bey
Total area: 42 m²
Contractor: SYCA
Client: Camper
Completion: 2012
Main materials: Panels of stretch fabric, Chipboard staircase, Acrylic painted floor
Site: Rue de la Republique 58, Lyon

CAMPER

（左頁）入り口より店内奥を見る

(Left page) Store interior viewed from the entrance

（上）床・壁の階段グラフィック

(Above) Stairs graphics on the walls and floor

（右）店内最奥部

(Right) Innermost part of the store

Sandworm

Installation architecture / Wenduine Beach, Belgium

Designer:
Marco Casagrande

Article: Yasuhiko Taguchi
Photography: Nikita Wu

ベルギーの水の都、ブルージュの近くにあるウィンドゥイネの砂丘にまるでスケールアウトしたゴカイ（サンド・ワーム）のようなオーガニックなストラクチャーがつくられた。このインスタレーションは長さが45m、高さと幅は10mあり、建築と環境アートの中間領域に位置する構造物である。

プロジェクトは、あらかじめ製作方法と、環境や景観などで地元との打ち合わせを入念に行い、結果、柳の枝だけで組み上げることになった。アーチストは融通性があって、オーガニックな存在で自然の一部となるような人工的なストラクチャーを「弱い建築」と定義し、これを作るために4週間、若い建築家そして地元の専門家のチームと協働した。

人々はこのスペースをピクニック、リラクゼーション、メディテーションの場として利用、ウィンドゥイネの干満のある海辺の敷地にマッチし、その地勢とうまく融合したこのストラクチャーを"柳のカテドラル"と呼んで親しんでいる。

「このゴカイの内部においてわれわれは光の陰影が作る自然のショーに迎えられる。人間の作った環境は人間性と自然界の仲介物になっている。その一部になるためには人間は弱くならなければならない」とピーター・バイエンは述べている。

Near Belgium's Venice of the North, Bruges, an organic structure, Sandworm, appeared on the dunes of the Wenduine coastline. This installation is 45 meters-long and 10 meters-wide and high, and occupies the space in between architecture and environmental art.

The structure is constructed completely of willow following the local knowledge of a continuing interaction between work and the environment. The designer defined a human-made structure that appears to become part of nature through flexibility and organic presence as "weak architecture," and worked with a team of young architects and local experts for four weeks to build the structure.

Visitors use this space for picnics, relaxation, and meditation. They liken Sandworm to a "willow cathedral" which is finely tuned to the site-specific conditions of the Wenduine tidal beaches.

Peter Beyen comments, "inside the Sandworm you are greeted by a natural spectacle of light and shadow. …The built human environment is a mediator between human nature and nature itself. To be part of this, man must be weak."

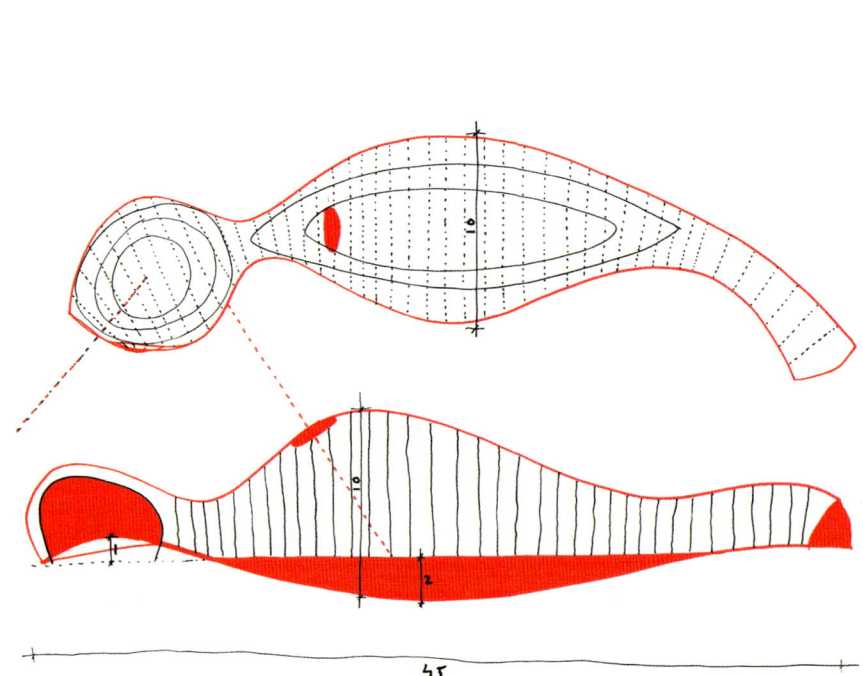

（左頁下）平断面ドローイング

(Left page bottom) Drawings of the plan
and section

（下）海岸の巨大なゴカイ

(Bottom) Huge sandworm on the dune
of the Wenduine coastline

柳の
カテドラル

（上）メインエントランス
(Above) Main entrance

（上）サブエントランス
(Above) Sub entrance

（右）ゴカイの内部
(Right) Interio view of the Sandworm

（上）ゴカイの内部

(Above) Interior view of the Sandworm

（下）制作風景

(Bottom) Production scene

Designer: Marco Casagrande
Organizer: Beaufort 04 Triennial of
Contemporary Art
Author: Marco Casagrande
Project manager: Nikita Wu / Casagrande
Laboratory
Casagrande Laboratory project team: Jan
Luksik, Jan Tyrpekl, Lukas Landa,
Zuzana Hanuskova
Willow Experts: Karol Jaworski, Pawel
Beaufort Specialists: Santiago De Waele,
Karel Van Kelst
Curator: Jonas Vandeghinste
Measures: 45 m long, 10 m wide, 10 m
high
Total area: 320 m²
Completion: Mar. 2012
Main materials: Willow, Sand
Site: Wenduine Beach, Belgium

Designers and
Architects' Portraits

Meyer en Van Schooten Architecten
Shoebaloo (p.148)

François Dumas - Studio François Dumas
Camper 20 Year (p.152)

**Katherine Kemp and Hanna Richardson -
Zwi Interiors Architecture**
11 Docklands pizzeria (p.142)

**Daniel Balo, Zsofi Dobos, Noemi Varga,
Dora Medveczky, Judit Emese Konopas**
Nanushka Beta Store (p.145)

Zaha Hadid - Zaha Hadid Architects
The Fudge (p.130)

Thom Mayne - Morphosis
Clyde Frazier (p.14)

Carmen Baselga
Paco Roncero's Workshop (p.122)

**António Fernandez, Ema Rosmaninho -
António Fernandez Architects**
É Prá Poncha (p.138)

Dan Brunn - Dan Brunn architect
Yojisan (p.36)

Lawrence Scarpa - Brooks Scarpa / Clearscapes
CAM Raleigh (p.94)

**Martin Ostermann, Lena Kleinheinz /
magma architecture**
Masrah Al Qasba (p.80)

Marco Casagrande
Sand Warm (p.160)

JL + MG - NAU
Raitteisen's flagship branch (p.110)

Nattapon Klinsuwan - NKDW
Chalachol Hair Salon (p.134)

Hulett Jones and Paul Haydu - jones l haydu
Coffe Bar (p.69)

Manuel Clavel Rojo - Clavel Arquitectos
Casanueva's Pharmacy (p.114)

Leendert Tange - Storeage
The Grapy Store (p.55)

Serie Architects
BMW (AG) (p.90)

SPA-DE

スペード Vol.19
Space & Design
International Review of Interior Design

発行日   2013年5月15日

編集人   藤井一比古
編　集   松本軍四郎　只井信子
アドヴァイザー　川床 優

アートディレクション　TAKAIYAMA inc.

発行者   松本軍四郎
発行所   有限会社ファーイースト・デザイン・エディターズ
         〒160-0023
         東京都新宿区西新宿3-5-3　西新宿ダイヤモンドパレス217号
         TEL 03-6279-4544　FAX 03-6279-4663
発売所   株式会社六耀社
         〒160-0022
         東京都新宿区新宿2-19-12　静岡銀行ビル5F
         TEL 03-3354-4020　FAX 03-3352-3106
         振替　00120-5-58856
         http://www.rikuyosha.co.jp
制作協力   株式会社乃村工藝社
印刷・製本 シナノ書籍印刷 株式会社

Printed in China
ISBN978-4-89737-747-6
無断転載・複写を禁じます。

Contributing Editors
荒　幾則（ロンドン）   Ikunori Ara (London)
田口泰彦（ニューヨーク）   Yasuhiko Taguchi (New York)
深沢正篤（ミラノ）   Masaatsu Fukazawa (Milano)

Translator
林　千根   Chine Hayashi

広告索引　Advertisement Index
002-003　サカイ　SAKAI Co.,Ltd
004　シーアイ化成　C.I.Kasei Co.,Ltd
005　乃村工藝社　NOMURA Co.,Ltd
166　マルモ出版　Marumo Publishing Co.,Ltd
167　ピーオーピー　POP Inc.

For this edition:
©2013 ARTPOWER

For the original edition:
©2013 Fareast Design Editors Inc

#217, 3-5-3 Nishi-shinjuku, Shinjuku-ku, Tokyo, JAPAN
Postal Code 160-0023
Phone: +81-3-6279-4544　FAX: +81-3-6279-4663
Publisher: Gunshiro Matsumoto
Executive Director: Kazuhiko Fujii
Editor: Gunshiro Matsumoto
Art Director: TAKAIYAMA inc.

Producer: RIKUYOSHA CO.,Ltd.
2-19-12,Shinjuku,Shinjuku-ku,Tokyo,JAPAN
Postal Code 160-0022
Phone: +81-3-3354-4020 FAX: +81-3-3352-3106
http://www.rikuyosha.co.jp

ARTPOWER
Room 13B, Zi Jing Ge, Fa Zhan Xing Yuan,
No. 1 Minitian Road, Futian, Shenzhen, China
Tel: +86-755-8291-3355　Fax: +86-755-8202-0029
http://www.artpower.com.cn
artpower@artpower.com.cn

Printed in China

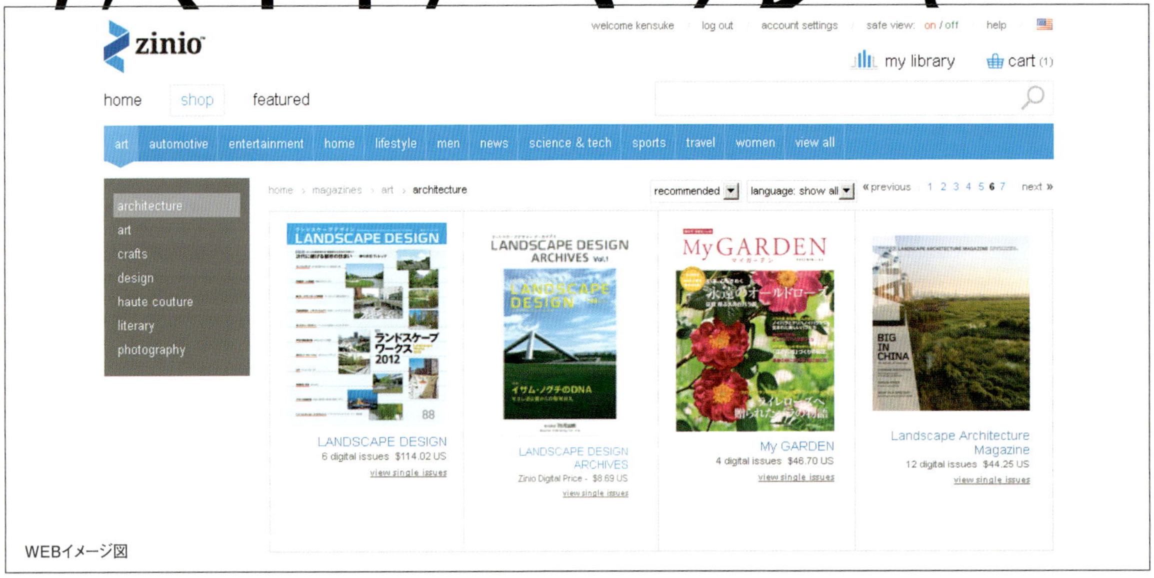

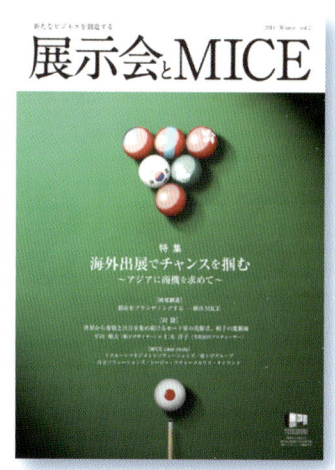

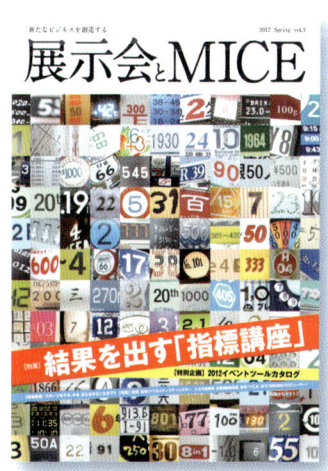

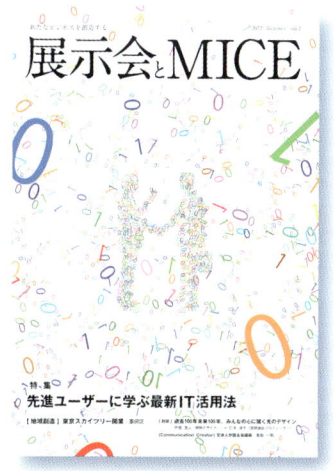

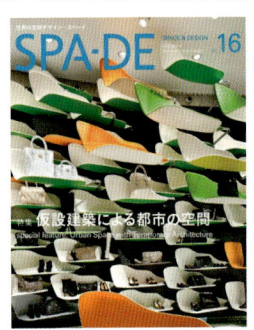
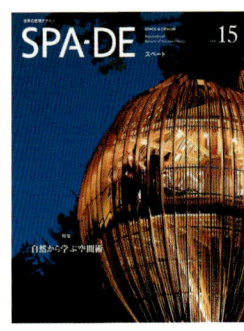
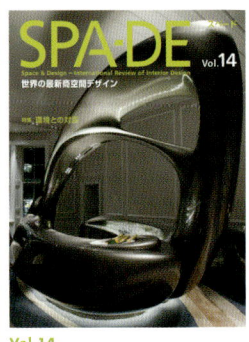

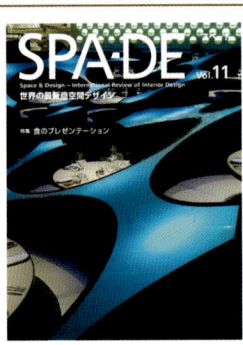
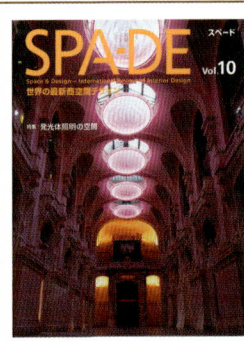
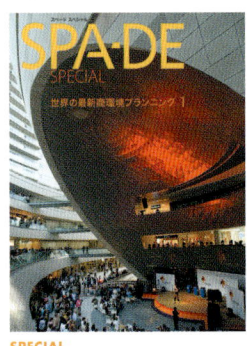

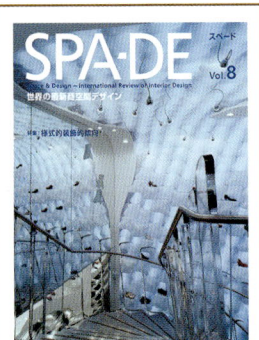
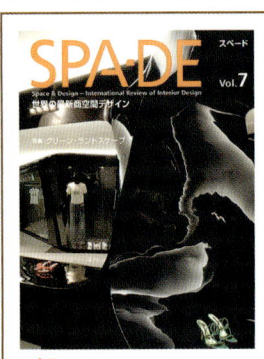
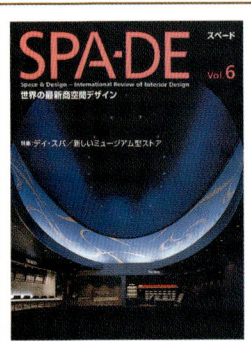
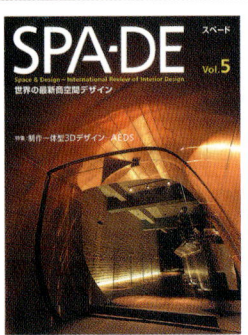